I Will Abolish the Bow

I Will Abolish the Bow

Christianity, Personhood,
and the End of Animal Exploitation

By
Matthew A. King

WIPF & STOCK · Eugene, Oregon

I WILL ABOLISH THE BOW
Christianity, Personhood, and the End of Animal Exploitation

Copyright © 2021 Matthew A. King. All rights reserved. Except for brief quotations in critical publications or reviews, no part of this book may be reproduced in any manner without prior written permission from the publisher. Write: Permissions, Wipf and Stock Publishers, 199 W. 8th Ave., Suite 3, Eugene, OR 97401.

Wipf & Stock
An Imprint of Wipf and Stock Publishers
199 W. 8th Ave., Suite 3
Eugene, OR 97401

www.wipfandstock.com

PAPERBACK ISBN: 978-1-6667-0027-5
HARDCOVER ISBN: 978-1-6667-0028-2
EBOOK ISBN: 978-1-6667-0029-9

Manufactured in the U.S.A.   JUNE 11, 2021

Scripture quotations are from the ESV® Bible (The Holy Bible, English Standard Version®), copyright © 2001 by Crossway, a publishing ministry of Good News Publishers. Used by permission. All rights reserved.

Scripture quotations marked (NLT) are taken from the Holy Bible, New Living Translation, copyright ©1996, 2004, 2015 by Tyndale House Foundation. Used by permission of Tyndale House Publishers, a Division of Tyndale House Ministries, Carol Stream, Illinois 60188. All rights reserved.

Scripture quotations from The Authorized (King James) Version. Rights in the Authorized Version in the United Kingdom are vested in the Crown. Reproduced by permission of the Crown's patentee, Cambridge University Press

Dedicated to Ripley and Zira, for helping me to understand.

Table of Contents

Acknowledgments ix
Introduction xi

1. Christianity's Failure to Address Animal Rights 1
2. Defining Biblical Personhood 8
3. Dominion 17
4. New Earth Abolition (NEA) 22
5. The Fate of Domesticated Animals 30
6. Addressing Abuse of the Bible 41
7. Addressing Speciesism 44
8. Animal Exploitation: A Biblical Regulation 52
9. Questions about Jesus 63
10. Questions about the Afterlife 78
11. Questions about Individual Passages 91
12. Questions about Nephesh Personhood 95
13. Questions about NEA 98

Epilogue 105
Resources for NEA 107
Bibliography 111
Subject Index 117
Scripture Index 123

Acknowledgments

I WANT TO THANK Bible Hub (https://biblehub.com/) for their tremendously helpful website. They have impressively cataloged every major translation that allows a side-by-side comparison of all of them. This web page makes for a quick and effective way for anyone to learn the many versions of the Bible.

I also want to thank several individuals for their guidance and help in my writing of this book. I greatly thank Pastor Frank Hoffman for his encouragement early on. Many thanks to Pastor Tony Cowley for his theological edits and tweaks. I very much appreciate the work of my editor, Christina Pfister, for her talented abilities in adjusting and fine-tuning this work.

I'm profoundly grateful to my brother-in-law, Samuel Cowley, for endlessly listening to the accuracy of the verses and citations.

Finally, I'd like to acknowledge my wife, Nina King, for always inspiring me, especially with this book. Her compassion is endless, and she always represents a radiant light in a dark world. Her encouragement and support led me to become an advocate for the animals.

Introduction

DID YOU EVER HAVE a Christian family member tell you that God wants you to eat meat? Have your Christian friends said that God does not care about animals? You are not alone. In our ministry, the Christian Animal Rights Association, we often hear from secular animal rights activists who want to believe in God, but find their own convictions regarding kindness to animals not reflected in the Christian faith. We also frequently meet Christian animal rights activists who see other Christians exploiting animals, but are unsure how to begin engaging in dialogue about it with them. How do they defend their principles when they will inevitably meet with resistance from their fellow believers? Perhaps you are a Christian wanting to know why animal rights issues are relevant to your faith. In this book, we attempt to address these issues and more.

If you ever felt marginalized by other Christians for your beliefs about animals, you are not alone, so do not lose hope. You will discover while reading this book that the Bible is an animal-rights-friendly text, and a strong case exists to support your compassionate convictions. Did you know the first animal rights activist was God himself? When he first formed the earth and all its inhabitants, he ordered humans to take good care of the animals and eat only plants (Genesis 1:20–30). Unfortunately, you have probably noticed that most Christians today do not acknowledge our God-mandated duties to animals, or if they do, they do so only to an inconsequential degree, amounting to no actual benefits to the animals themselves.

From Welfare to Rights

My wife and I formed the Christian Animal Rights Association in 2019, feeling there was a need for an organization in the Christian community with an uncompromising method of addressing the massive amount of exploitation and harm done to animals. We felt called to advance the cause of animals from one of welfare to rights. Welfare views animals as subservient, permitting humans to "humanely" (whatever that means) do as they please with them. Rights, instead, declares that animals are intrinsically valuable and exist with importance beyond and regardless of how humans may view them. Thus, our ministry believes the Christian perspective on animal rights at a minimum should be one of abolition, the goal being the end of animal exploitation. There is no right or humane way to harmfully exploit. Understanding this is the most necessary step in how Christians should view and treat animals.

Addressing Property Status – Personhood

However, our organization's goal goes beyond abolition. We strive for humans to live in harmony with animals as our Creator intended. Currently, animals are afforded no protections beyond property status. Treated as commodities, they are bought, sold, traded, and stolen. Just like clothing and stereos, animals have virtually no rights except that some of them are not to be treated cruelly. Arbitrary laws founded on human value do provide some minimal protections for a few fortunate species, but not for others. For instance, a 2019 federal law addressing animal cruelty applies to companion animals, but not to animals used for food or experimentation.[1] This incongruency further supports the idea that only select animals deserve compassion while others should be ignored.

---

1. Knowles and Mettler, "Trump Ban on Animal Cruelty."

INTRODUCTION

Property status is the fundamental problem with all human–animal interactions. Our ministry believes the best way to defeat this notion publicly, academically, and legally, is to fight against the property status of animals and defend and support their standing as persons. Christians in support of animal personhood view animals as persons instead of resources or property. In the court of law, you cannot have any rights unless you are deemed a person. Animals gaining legal personhood status may potentially allow them representation under the law for their interests. The legal interests of animals could include freedom from harm, confinement, and exploitation.

I wrote this book because, in all of my research, I realized historical Christianity had failed to provide a framework of personhood for animals. This failure helps perpetuate their property status, cementing them as resources instead of individuals worthy of moral consideration in basic interests. In this book, I attempt to define how the Bible determines personhood. I will further argue that Christians, activists or not, should acknowledge this animal personhood, and thus seek to end animal exploitation.

New Earth Abolition (NEA)

To formulate a more biblically accurate and compassionate way of acknowledging animal personhood, I have devised a method and a system of ethics based on scriptural principles, which combine the teachings of Jesus and biblical ideals. I have dubbed this method New Earth Abolition (NEA), a practice in which one lives by God's ultimate will and is morally considerate of his animal creations. NEA is an expression of why the Christian Animal Rights Association was formed in the first place. The principles of NEA seek to change humanity's relationship with animals from one of exploitation to one of serving. NEA draws its vision by way of reference to the ideal conditions seen on the New Earth, which will be inaugurated when Jesus returns, as suggested in Isaiah 11:6–9, Isaiah 65:25, and Hosea 2:18. These verses and the concept of NEA

INTRODUCTION

describe humans and animals living peacefully together without any form of exploitation. Utilizing the principles of NEA, our ministry seeks to change laws for animals. Through NEA, we also advocate that Christians discontinue the use of products and services that harm animals, and thus replace them with ethical alternatives.

Our ministry's greatest hope is to see humans and animals living in peaceful harmony with one another. With this book and its concepts as a guide, we hope eventually, Christians will see animals in a different light. We hope that Christians will no longer see animals as property or as commodities, but rather as God sees them: Persons–individuals with a unique personality entitled to lawful moral consideration. By seeing animals as people, we hope that Christianity will eliminate its current track record of exploitation and domination.

Summary

Within the first chapter, the book provides an examination of why Christianity has not been animal rights friendly. Chapters 2 through 5 assert our organization's foundational principles. Chapter 2 focuses on how the Bible defines personhood. Chapter 3 discusses how our ministry interprets the famous biblical word, "dominion." Chapter 4 centers on our application of New Earth Abolition (NEA). Chapter 5 demonstrates a biblical perspective on how our ministry views domesticated animals and how that differs from traditional, secular animal rights activism. Chapters 6 through 8 examine some of the biblical principles our organization takes into consideration when we interpret God's word. Chapter 6 advocates using the Bible to fight oppression rather than as a tool for torment. Chapter 7 examines how the Bible condemns all oppressive forms of discrimination, including speciesism. Chapter 8 examines how exploitation of animals is biblically regulated, not endorsed. Chapters 9 through 11 discuss common questions Christian animal rights activists, animal rights activists exploring Christianity, or Christians exploring animal rights may have. Chapter 9 equips activists with rebuttals to questions about

INTRODUCTION

Jesus and how he interacted with or what he taught about animals. Chapter 10 offers refutations of common arguments that exclude animals from the afterlife. Chapter 11 gives rebuttals to questions about individual passages commonly abused to justify atrocities committed against animals. Chapters 12 and 13 address some issues the reader may have regarding our principles. Chapter 12 presents common questions and our answers regarding nephesh personhood. Chapter 13 attempts to answer common questions we receive about NEA. Finally, the book closes out with resources to help implement NEA for Christians interested in beginning animal rights activism.

In order to better equip current animal rights activists or activist-interested readers with all of this knowledge, we must first look at the past and see how we got here. Animal rights has not been a concern historically because, in biblical times, humans had not dominated the earth like we have today. Wild animals were far more prevalent and posed a considerable danger at all times, which is unlike how most of humanity experiences life today. For instance, Leviticus 26:22 and Ezekiel 5:17 prophesy wild beasts killing children. Snakes, in particular, were dreaded (Numbers 21:6; Deuteronomy 32:24; Job 20:16; Jeremiah 8:17). Several Psalms reveal the dread of lions in metaphors (Psalm 7:2, 10:9, 17:12, 22:13, 22:21). Jackals seemed to be particularly feared (Isaiah 13:22; Jeremiah 9:11, 10:22; 49:33, 51:37; Malachi 1:3). Animals were not very esteemed because they represented a threat. Despite this anxiety, many passages predicted a time when humans and animals would live in peace (Job 5:22–23). Similarly, in the past, the exploitation of animals was necessary for survival. Today, the vast majority of modern industrialized cultures no longer need to exploit animals. Within this context, the first chapter is an attempt to uncover why Christianity has minimally addressed animal rights over the course of more than 2,000 years.

1

Christianity's Failure to Address Animal Rights

ONE PRIMARY REASON PARTICULAR religions or philosophies flourish is because they provide answers to the problems of their day. In John 9:5, Jesus described himself as the light of the world. He described his disciples with the same phrase in Matthew 5:14. While Christianity has been successful at bringing people to know Jesus, it has failed morally. When factoring in the idolatrous prosperity gospel, the alignment of Christianity with nationalism, and especially the recent Catholic sex scandals, I think that Christians, including myself, need to step back and ask ourselves: Are we the light of the world?

Christianity, like all religions, challenges the many problems of our day. Think of faith as being similar to fire. A flame can provide warmth on a cold day. Fire can cook food to relieve hunger and be harnessed as a means of protection. However, if one is not careful, it can burn the house down. Christianity can be used to light the way toward a brighter tomorrow or create the ashes from a societal inferno. Christianity, in recent times, has a track record of self-serving and egocentric thinking. However, Jesus taught us to be servants (Matthew 23:11), and Philippians 2:3 reminds us to count others as more significant than ourselves.

I Will Abolish the Bow

In contrast, historical Christianity helped relieve sociopolitical ills and encouraged human flourishing. Even recent American Christianity succeeded at helping relieve social troubles. Just look at the many universities and hospitals founded by believers and named after Christian saints. The Christian faith was especially helpful in the late 1800s to early 1900s when the Social Gospel emerged, spurring a movement to address complications from the Second American Industrial Revolution and its application of Social Darwinism. The Social Gospel sought to relieve poverty, deplorable slums, alcoholism, crime, and many other societal problems. The Young Men's Christian Association (YMCA) and the Salvation Army were associated with the Social Gospel.

The current state of Catholicism can be considered a textbook example of what happens when organized religion refuses to adapt. The Catholic Church, once seen as a bastion of American morality and ethical teaching, is now known more for its justification of priestly perpetrators than for defending the sexually abused victims. It is no wonder that most U.S. millennials and zoomers (Generation Z) do not identify with Christianity.[1] Some of that has to do with secular teaching in schools and colleges, but the primary blame can be placed on Christianity's current stance of anti-progressivism. The church has mostly aligned itself with conservative values and often impedes progress, especially when it comes to the equal treatment of others. It seems the church and its believers are not committed to improving the world, but are rather more interested in hindering advancement. Any and perhaps all attempts at relieving oppression and suffering from a Christian perspective are surprisingly criticized and labeled socialist, not by secular society, but by believers of the Christian faith.

Abortion is a complex issue that cannot be resolved with one comprehensive solution. I think the long-standing Christian pro-life position is an admirable one, though. In light of 1 Corinthians 10:24 stating, "Let no one seek his own good, but the good of his neighbor", I am hard-pressed not to agree that pro-life Christians have a point. They are considering others and the consequences of

---

1. Morrow, "Gen Z Biblical Worldview."

their actions. However, most United States Evangelicals, with their combined Christian-American values at hand, rarely consider how their actions affect others. Issues that affect the homeless, the environment, and animals are casually dismissed and declared liberal, while the fetus gets the utmost priority. If Christians took the other problems of the world half as seriously as they do abortion, we would be living in a far better place. Christianity needs a revival. Christians have become so inwardly focused on salvation, yet forget the kind words and actions of Jesus. Christianity needs to recover social influence and revive the spirit of Jesus, the spirit of loving one's neighbor.

Not surprisingly, animal rights is a largely ignored issue within the church. Christianity, in my experience, is almost entirely hostile to animal rights. While exhibiting for the Christian Vegetarian Association and after forming the Christian Animal Rights Association, I have noticed a common theme when speaking to patrons at vegan festivals: They are often former Christians. When asked about their lapse, most of them respond by saying that either their parents told them the Bible says you should/have to eat animals or some form of the argument declaring that humans have dominion over the animals. The church's indifference to the plight of animals may be the greatest indictment against modern Christianity. Yearly, over 70 billion land-dwelling animals are killed worldwide for food.[2] They are crowded into filthy cages, mercilessly killed, and given not one measure of compassion or kindness, despite humanity being able to live perfectly fine and even thrive without the flesh of animals. Much of Christianity's disregard toward animals may be because of Charles Darwin and his theory of evolution by natural selection.

Delusions of Darwinism

One of Christianity's primary objections to animal rights is based on the misguided notion that it is interconnected with Darwinism.

---

2. Sanders, "Global Animal Slaughter Statistics."

Anything associated with Darwin and his theories is dismissed as secular or even sinister. When Christian apologists speak of animal rights, it is usually considered a logical implication of Darwinism and evolutionary theory. Here are a couple of examples:

> Second, observe that the animal rights agenda is rooted in a Darwinian evolutionary worldview. If all creatures and plants are merely evolved species, then one is not "superior" to another—just different. Hence, a rose and a scorpion are as valuable and worthy of care as a human baby or a bull. This inane thinking is the direct result of buying into the thoroughly debunked theory of evolution and dismissing the abundant evidence in the created order of a supernatural Creator Who has revealed Himself to humans via nature and His written Word in the Bible.
> —Dave Miller, PhD, "Humans are Not Animals"[3]

> As a matter of fact, that is precisely the rationale behind the modern animal-rights movement, a movement whose raison d'être is the utter degradation of the human race. Naturally, all radical animal-rights advocates are evolutionists. Their belief system is an inevitable byproduct of evolutionary theory.
> —John MacArthur, "Putting Humans in Their Place"[4]

This association of Darwinism with evil is worthy of acknowledgment. Charles Darwin's theory of evolution popularized after the publication of his *On the Origin of Species*. Unfortunately, Darwin's concepts were abused during the Second American Industrial Revolution, which sparked Social Darwinism, in which the poor were viewed as inferior. The wealthier classes saw poverty as a hindrance to progress and thus saw the underprivileged as unworthy of help. In this line of thinking, the poor, sick, and disabled are the weak, holding back the strong, capable humans who contribute to society.

---

3. Miller, "Humans Are Not Animals."
4. MacArthur, "Putting Humans in Their Place."

Social Darwinism desires for the strong to prosper and for the weak to perish. Based on the social application of Darwin's theories, animal rights certainly do not fall in line with the ideas of Social Darwinism. A Social Darwinist would declare their own supremacy and that every creature "below" them is weak and must serve the stronger humans. The caring, concern, and benevolence that animal rights espouses is not like Darwinism at all. Instead, it is the traditional, harmful Christian teachings about animal rights adopted by many Christians, including Miller and MacArthur quoted above, that are far more Darwinist, as they imply humans to be superior, and animals to be weak. Animal rights is a generous and charitable cause. Charity is not a teaching of Darwinism. Charity is a teaching of Christianity as Acts 20:35 declares, "In all things I have shown you that by working hard in this way we must help the weak and remember the words of the Lord Jesus, how he himself said, 'It is more blessed to give than to receive.'" Christians condemn Darwinism, yet they oppress animals. They imply that humans are strong, and the animals weak, yet ironically declare animal rights advocates Darwinist. Paradoxically, animal rights activists, who are usually not Christian, are often unwittingly operating by the biblical principles of protecting the weak (Psalm 82:3-4) and defending the oppressed (Proverbs 31:8-9). However, not all of Christianity has been hostile, and there has been some concern for animals.

Christianity and Animal Rights

Animal welfare has a storied, albeit relatively minor, history in the church. Consider the well-known verse Proverbs 12:10, which condemns cruelty to animals. Catholic St. Francis of Assisi is famously known for his friendship with animals. The most influential Christian animal rights figure has been Reverend Andrew Linzey, who discussed the moral consideration of animals from a Christian perspective with *theos-rights*; a term that was coined by Linzey in his work, *Christianity and the Rights of Animals*. Linzey states, "According to theos-rights what we do to animals is not simply a matter of taste or convenience or philanthropy. When we speak of animal rights we conceptualize what is objectively owed to animals as a matter of justice by virtue of their Creator's right. Animals can be wronged because their Creator can be wronged in his creation."[5] Linzey's work is important and thought-provoking. His work is mostly deontological, which means his ethics are based on a set of rules. He states that animals have rights because their Creator, the rule maker, demands these rights. His work is incredibly important to me as he was one of the few Christian authors who had books and information discussing the rights of animals. Unfortunately, his work is mostly unknown to believers because Christianity is often hostile to animal rights. Thus, activists frequently turn to secular teachings.

Secular Teachings and Animal Rights

Secular utilitarian philosopher Peter Singer in *Animal Liberation* refers to the principle of equal consideration of interests for animals.[6] I understand this to mean wherever human and animal interests are similar, they should be treated the same. For instance, humans and animals both experience pain. Just like we would not inflict pain on a human for trivial reasons, we also should not inflict pain on animals for trivial reasons.

United States philosopher Tom Regan discussed the issue in *The Case for Animal Rights*. He states that animals ethically matter because they are subjects-of-a-life, which he describes as the criteria for accepting an individual into moral consideration. Subjects-of-a-life have certain mental qualifications like emotions, desires, and other complex attributes. Regan believed every healthy developed mammal fits this term and thus have intrinsic value and rights. Accordingly, humans have a responsibility to give animals equal consideration and not disturb their lives.[7]

---

5. Linzey, *Christianity and the Rights of Animals*, 97
6. Singer, *Animal Liberation*, 7
7. Regan, "Subject-Of-A-Life."

Regan and Singer's approaches have become influential in the modern animal rights movement. These approaches are excellent in establishing criteria for why animals deserve rights from a secular perspective. However, the primary problem with Linzey, Singer, and Regan's approaches is that they do little to biblically challenge the property status of animals, as far as I can tell. The Christian Animal Rights Association believes the most effective way to challenge this property status is to establish the personhood of animals. Our next chapter delves into a discussion on the biblical definition of personhood. Secular philosophy has approached animal personhood, but Christian philosophy has only minimally discussed this subject.

2

Defining Biblical Personhood

PERSONHOOD IS DIFFICULT TO define because it has around five definitions depending on the context. The word is defined through political, economic, social, religious, and legal understandings.[1] The definition of personhood I want to focus on is in the religious sense by examining how the Bible defines personhood. By first defining biblical personhood, this understanding can then be applied legally. This legal application would then redefine personhood in political, economic, and social contexts.

Personhood is described by dictionary.com as the state or fact of being a person.[2] Lexico Dictionary defines a person as a human being regarded as an individual.[3] This definition reflects the current conviction that persons are strictly humans. However, this was not always the case. For instance, the U.S. Constitution previously rejected personhood status for Black slaves.[4] The United States Supreme Court denied personhood status to women in the past.[5] How society defines a person is constantly being debated. In my definition, a person is an individual who is entitled to ethical

1. Vandenboom, et al., "A Deeper Look into Personhood."
2. Dictionary.com, LLC, "Personhood," definition 1.
3. Lexico.com, "Person," definition 1.
4. Waggoner, "Let's Talk about Legal 'Personhood.'"
5. Cobb, "Women's 'Legal Personhood.'"

and legal consideration. However, the current collective definitions of personhood exclude animals from that notion. Secular philosophy has tried to define a less rigid definition of personhood that is not based on species membership, just like previous definitions excluded based on race and sex.

Secular Definitions of Personhood

Secular philosophy has discussed animal personhood. Primatologist Dawn Prince-Hughes believes gorillas meet personhood criteria. Reporter Jennifer Langston summarized Prince-Hughes's criterions, stating, "In her view, that includes exhibiting morality, having a concept of the past and future, an ability to understand complex rules and their consequences on an emotional level."[6] I consider these criteria to be inadequate as it seems most animals, and even some humans, lack some of these characteristics.

Law professor Gary L. Francione believes the only requirement for personhood is sentience.[7] Francione's view is the best secular position in my opinion because it is most inclusive, as this would also include mentally disabled, very young, and demented, elderly humans, for example. It can be applied to all sentient animals, regardless of their intelligence. This notion closely coincides with the biblical definition of personhood, as I will demonstrate in the coming paragraphs. However, historically, Christianity has not acknowledged this definition of personhood.

Nephesh Personhood

To my knowledge, the issue of animal personhood has not yet been discussed from a Christian perspective. The logical implication of acknowledging animal personhood is not merely animal welfare, but rather animal rights, which means humans can no longer use them in industry. The legal term personhood has been featured

6. Langston, "Gorilla Touched Her Soul."
7. Shooster, "Legal Personhood and Rights of Wild Animals."

as an important element in the debate over the issue of abortion. Many Christians believe abortion is sinful because several biblical verses suggest personhood begins before birth (Psalm 139:13, Jeremiah 1:5). Since these verses imply personhood, most pro-life Christians agree with legislation that assigns personhood and legal protection to the fetus. Many Christian organizations have developed legal strategies to fight for fetal rights based on the premise of personhood. Within this book, I do not intend to argue when personhood begins, but rather who qualifies as a person. First, we must determine what personhood means in the Christian sense:

Roman philosopher and politician Boethius described a person as "an individual substance of a rational nature." Theologian and priest Thomas Aquinas also rejected irrational beings from personhood.[8] I find this definition problematic, as it implies that humans who are irrational, such as the mentally disabled, children, or demented elderly, are excluded from moral consideration. Modern attempts to define personhood often rely on defining it with the strict human characteristic of being made in the image of God (Genesis 1:26-27). However, this term in context does not appear to denote personhood, but rather human responsibility. I will discuss this in later chapters.

Biblically, I propose a better definition in which all humans can be declared persons because of one particular characteristic, the Hebrew term *nephesh chayyah*. This word, *nephesh*, in particular, has an interpretation history that makes the word's exact definition hard to determine in translation. Within the Old Testament, the word appears more than 700 times. Depending on the context, the word *nephesh* can have different meanings. The Bible Project reasons that *nephesh*, in its simplest form, means the English word "throat." As everything about one's life relies on the throat (eating, drinking, breathing), *nephesh* can "...refer to the whole person."[9]

The reader can see this word used differently throughout the Bible depending on the translation. In Genesis 2:7 (NLT), Adam became a *nephesh chayyah*, translated as "a living person."

---

8. New Catholic Encyclopedia. "Person (In Philosophy)."
9. Bible Project, "Nephesh: 'Soul'", 1-2.

Defining Biblical Personhood

A *nephesh met* or "dead person" is described in Numbers 6:6 (NASB). *Nephesh* is also used in the plural as Deuteronomy 10:22 states there were *shiv'im nephesh* or "seventy persons." Jeremiah 52:30 describes *yehudim nephesh* or "Judean persons." With the use of these descriptors before or after *nephesh*, the word is perhaps best understood as person (plural: persons). Strangely, the only English Bible translation that uses the term person in Genesis 2:7 is the New Living Translation (NLT). Other translations use the term "creature" (ESV, YLT), "being" (NIV, BSB, NASB, NKJV, CSB, HCSB, ISV, NET, AFV, GWT, NAS 77), or "soul" (KJB, NHEB, JPST 1917, KJB 2000, AKJV, ASV, BST, DRB, DBT, ERV, WBT, WEB). Nevertheless, this definition of personhood refers to God breathing characteristics of a person into Adam, essentially forming a personality. Each human has their own distinctive, individual personality.

Humans are Persons

We can consider all humans persons because they are *nephesh chayyah* (Genesis 2:7). This Hebrew term is the defining characteristic of a person. By using the term *nephesh chayyah*, the Bible makes it clear who is defined as a person from a Christian perspective. This designation gives Christians a way to approach the law by advocating personhood be awarded to all humans — regardless of race, sex, or any other difference. In the United States, you do not have any constitutional rights unless you are a person. Legally speaking, a natural person (as opposed to legal persons such as governments and businesses) is formally described as a living human being by the Legal Information Institute.[10] Natural persons in the United States are entitled to constitutional rights, to life, and liberty. The 13th amendment abolished human slavery. The 14th amendment guarantees equal protection under the law. These laws and many others apply to all humans because they are natural persons.

---

10. Legal Information Institute, "Natural Person."

Animals are Persons (People), Too

As iterated earlier, possessing the attribute of *nephesh chayyah* indicates that someone is a person. In the New Living Translation (NLT), *nephesh* was translated as "person" for humans in Genesis 2:7. Animals matter to God because they also possess this moniker of personhood. Even though *nephesh chayyah* describes both humans (Genesis 2:7) and animals (Genesis 1:20, 21, 24, 30, 2:19) in the original Hebrew, the meaning has been lost in translation. Strangely, the New Living Translation (NLT) does not use the term person to describe animals in Genesis 1:20; 21; 24; 30; and 2:19 like it does for humans in 2:7. Animals should also be considered persons too, based on the original Hebrew. I can only speculate, but it seems the translators wanted to disregard animals in this designation of personhood. God's declaration of animals as persons makes sense, as each animal has their own unique personality. Any human that cares for animals can tell you this is true.

Animals fit the criterion for personhood as they also possess *nephesh chayyah*. Again, this Hebrew term describes both animals (Genesis 1:20, 21, 24, 30, 2:19) and humans (Genesis 2:7) in the garden of Eden. The Bible makes it clear in these passages who is a person from a Christian perspective. Christians should seek to change the way U.S. and worldwide laws are interpreted for animals based on this understanding. This Christian understanding of personhood conflicts with the laws currently in place regarding animals. Generally, animals have no legal status beyond property value assigned by humans. Christians should support the notion that animals be recognized under the law as persons, as the Bible views them. By definition, animals would not qualify as natural persons in the U.S. because of their species membership. However, animals can certainly be considered legal persons.

The Legal Information Institute defines a "legal person" as a human or non-human entity that is treated as a person for limited legal purposes.[11] Legal persons are not humans, but are still granted rights, depending on situation and necessity. For instance,

---

11. Legal Information Institute, "Legal Person."

Defining Biblical Personhood

corporations and government agencies are granted personhood status despite obviously not being natural persons. Granting animals personhood status would only provide them considerations where applicable. Animals could be afforded rights only in terms of their interests, like avoiding pain and the right to bodily integrity. Animals have been recognized as legal persons in two states within India, which grants them some legal protection, rights, and justice.[12] As of this writing, the United States have yet to recognize an animal as a legal person. However, the secular Nonhuman Rights Project is working to institute this status of legal personhood for certain animals.[13] The also secular Animal Legal Defense Fund promotes a recognition similar to legal personhood for animals.[14] The Christian Animal Rights Association also advocates for the legal personhood of animals based on the awareness of *nephesh chayyah*.

Scientific Evidence

This designation of personhood in the Bible is more than just a word. *Nephesh* appears to apply to the aspect of sentience. Lexico Dictionary defines "sentient" as able to perceive or feel things.[15] Over 2,500 studies show that animals are sentient.[16] Obviously, humans are also sentient. Thus, animals may feel and perceive the world similarly, if not the same, as humans do. *Nephesh* not only implies sentience, but also personality. It is no coincidence the word "person" is so closely associated with personality. Psychology Today defines "personality" as a person's distinctive patterns of thinking, feeling, and behaving.[17]

---

12. Raja, "All Animals Are 'Legal Persons.'"
13. Nonhuman Rights Project, "Litigation."
14. Animal Legal Defense Fund, "Animals' Legal Status."
15. Lexico.com, "Sentient."
16. Bekoff, "2,500 Studies Declare Animal Sentience."
17. Psychology Today, "Personality."

I Will Abolish the Bow

Calling animals persons indicates that they have unique personalities, which is confirmed by scientific evidence. For instance, Genesis 1:20 designates *nephesh chayyah* to fish. A 2017 report showed that fish have distinct and intricate personalities.[18] Genesis 1:21 assigns *nephesh chayyah* to great sea creatures, such as whales. A 2011 study revealed that sperm whales possess unique personalities.[19] Genesis 1:20–21 implies *nephesh chayyah* toward birds (later confirmed in Genesis 1:30 and 2:19–20). A 2011 study showed that birds have diverse personalities.[20] Genesis 1:24 attaches *nephesh chayyah* to livestock (translated from the Hebrew term for cattle), which is presumably common farm animals like cows, pigs, and chickens. A 2017 examination of research demonstrated cows have individual personalities and a vast emotional range.[21] A 2015 review of studies revealed that pigs are smart, emotional, and have distinctive personalities.[22] A 2017 study analysis of chickens revealed that they possess unique personalities.[23] Genesis 1:24 also attributes *nephesh chayyah* to creeping things, which I presume are beings like rodents, lizards, and amphibians. A 2019 report proved that mice have distinctive personalities.[24] A 2006 investigation indicated lizards possess personalities and some enjoy socializing.[25] Salamanders are a type of amphibian. These creatures were shown to possess personalities in a 2018 study.[26] Genesis 1:24 also attaches *nephesh chayyah* to the beasts of the earth. I presume this refers to wild animals of the forests and fields. A 2019 review of research indicates that deer possess distinct personalities.[27] Similarly, a

---

18. University of Exeter, "Fish Have Complex Personalities."
19. Braconnier, "Sperm Whales Individual Personalities."
20. University of York. "Animals Have Personalities, Too."
21. Bekoff, "Cows: Bright Emotional Individuals."
22. Bekoff, "Pigs Intelligent, Emotional, Cognitively Complex."
23. Springer, "Think Chicken: Intelligent, Caring, and Complex."
24. ISRAEL21c Staff, "Mice Have Personality."
25. Khamsi, "Lizards Have Personalities Too."
26. Piatek, "Salamanders with Personality."
27. Samuel, "Whitetail Bucks Have Different Personalities?"

Defining Biblical Personhood

2018 study exhibited that elephants possess individual personalities.[28] Genesis 1:30 then declares all previously mentioned animals as having *nephesh chayyah*. Finally, Genesis 2:19-20 attributes *nephesh chayyah* to livestock, birds, and beasts of the field. These were the animals Adam named. The biblical designation of *nephesh chayyah* demonstrates what science has produced volumes in confirming, that animals are sentient and possess unique personalities all their own.

Observational Evidence

In my own personal experience before about the age of 23, I had always thought what philosopher René Descartes concluded, which was that animals were like machines. That by instinct, they simply existed, ate, defecated, and copulated, with little desire for anything more. Most of this was because I did not grow up with animals. As newlyweds, my wife brought home a Shetland sheepdog whom we affectionately dubbed Ripley. It was then I discovered so much about animals I never knew. While feeding him a dog food mixed with peas and carrots, I noticed when I would pick up the container; the bowl would have a few peas at the bottom after he was finished eating. This happened every time I fed him. Then I noticed one day while watching him eat that he was spitting out the peas! I found he had a real preference for the carrots and the rest of the food, but had a serious dislike of the little green foodstuff. Just like I do not like brussels sprouts, Ripley had a preference too! It was then, and after many more observations, that I realized animals have unique personalities and individual preferences. They are not just a *something*; there is a *someone* behind those eyes.

Acknowledging this biblical, scientific, and observational awareness of the personhood of animals should cause us to pause and reflect on humanity's treatment of them. Embedded in the context of Genesis 1:20 through 2:20, there is an acknowledgment

---

28. O'Neill, "Elephants Have Distinct Personalities."

of this personhood of both animals and humans. Also included within the text is Genesis 1:26, which mentions the famous word, *dominion*. This term and its interpretation is critical to understanding the Christian perspective on animal rights. Our next chapter focuses on this word and its logical implications.

3

Dominion

THE TERM *DOMINION* IS found in Genesis 1:26, which states, "Then God said, 'Let us make man in our image, after our likeness. And let them have dominion over the fish of the sea and over the birds of the heavens and over the livestock and over all the earth and over every creeping thing that creeps on the earth.'" Dominion is one of the most frequent words Christians use to justify atrocities against animals. Christians often interpret the word to mean one of tyranny or domination over animals, often likening the term to one of ruthless exploitation. Our ministry has spoken to many former Christians who said a family member told them dominion meant they could eat animals. I even had a family member tell me she thought dominion meant discretion, likening it to humans doing whatever they want to animals with impunity.

Dominion in Context

Dominion must be seen in its context of Genesis 1:20–30, which depicts God's original and idyllic intention of humanity living in peace and harmony with animals in the garden of Eden. Importantly, in Genesis 1:29–30, God commands both humans and animals to eat only the plants. Genesis 1:20–30 is obviously the ideal, as evidenced by God calling the garden of Eden very good in Genesis 1:31. So clearly, dominion does not mean using animals as food. God's ideal was obviously that humans and animals live together in peaceful coexistence, with humans caring for animals. Implicitly, I think we can safely assume dominion also does not mean harmfully exploiting animals in any way, including for experimentation, fashion, or entertainment. Furthermore, our ministry understands biblical dominion to be like the leadership of a good king stewarding those under his rule. Psalm 72:8 specifically uses the term dominion. Psalm 72:1–17 defines the character of a righteous king. Verse 7 states, "In his days may the righteous flourish, and peace abound, till the moon be no more!" Then in verse 12, "For he delivers the needy when he calls, the poor and him who has no helper." Finally, in verse 13, "He has pity on the weak and the needy, and saves the lives of the needy." Significantly, Psalm 72 is a prophecy about Jesus as king.

Jesus is a good king, and we should apply his example of dominion to animals by displaying what he showed humans: compassion (Luke 7:13). Based on Jesus' teachings, we should aspire to be peacemakers (Matthew 5:9) and be merciful (Matthew 5:7). Jesus identified with the weak and oppressed and said that his followers should help those in need as if he were one of the oppressed (Matthew 25:40). Importantly, he had three particular teachings that detail humanity's proper dominion over animals.

The Golden Rule

Jesus taught the Golden Rule in Matthew 7:12, stating, "So whatever you wish that others would do to you, do also to them, for this is the Law and the Prophets." Similarly, Luke 6:31 states, "And as you wish that others would do to you, do so to them." When we bring animals into moral consideration, are we treating animals as we want to be treated? If we treat animals the way we would want to be treated, we would have to stop torturing them for food, experiments, and entertainment, to name but a few examples. Would you want to be treated like an animal in any industry? Of course, you would not. No one would. Thus, treating animals with the Golden Rule means refraining from harmfully exploiting them in any way.

The Second Great Commandment

Jesus' First Great Commandment was stated in Matthew 22:37. Jesus followed that with the Second Great Commandment in Matthew 22:39, which states, "And a second is like it: You shall love your neighbor as yourself." The Second Great Commandment is the portion I want to focus on here. This teaching is similar to the Golden Rule in that they both teach egalitarianism, a belief that beings should be treated with equality. Looking specifically at the teaching, we obviously cannot love our neighbors, the animals, as ourselves, when we are causing them harm to satisfy nothing more than taste and pleasure. No one would ever want to be treated like an animal stuck at a farm or laboratory, where their existence is commodified, and their pain and suffering are not considered. Thus, anything we would not do to a human, we should not do to an animal in terms where they are similar.

Servanthood

There is a pericope in John 13:12–14 in which Jesus washes his disciples' feet. Humans often wore sandals while walking through the desert 2,000 years ago. When a man or woman would go inside of the house, they would need to wipe off their feet to remove the sand and dirt that was baked on them from the hot sun. The lowest servant would often have the job of washing feet, which was considered a demeaning task. Jesus washed his disciples' feet, humbling himself, taking the role of a servant. He commands us to become servants, as well.

When looking at how Jesus' teaching on servanthood relates to animals, we are not just supposed to treat them as equals. We are actually to regard them as more important than ourselves (Philippians 2:3). You have probably heard Christians say that animals were put here for humans. Following Jesus' teaching on servanthood, animals were not put here to serve us. Humans were put here to serve animals. I interpret this to be confirmed by Mark 9:35, where Jesus declared, "If anyone would be first, he must be last of all and *servant of all*."

Finally, 1 John 2:6 instructs us to live like Jesus. This verse corresponds with Genesis 1:26, stating that humans were made in the image of God, as Jesus declared, "I and the Father are one." (John 10:30). When paired in context with dominion, our ministry interprets the image of God to mean humans are to mirror the behavior God shows towards those who are under his rule. Thus, the image of God ideally entails humans having responsibility. The Christian Animal Rights Association honors this by applying Jesus' principles regarding equality and servanthood to help guide human behavior toward animals. The Christian Animal Rights Association believes equality and servanthood are the most important ethics when determining how humans show dominion as image-bearers of God.

Future Prophecies about Harmony with Animals

The most important contextual detail about dominion is understanding the harmonious relationship seen in Eden. As previously discussed, the garden of Eden was the perfect place, where none of the terrible things we encounter in this life even existed. Genesis 1:20–30 indicates that God intended all animals and humans to live eternally in good health and vitality together, with all enjoying the company of each other and only eating plants. The disobedience of Adam and Eve brought all sorts of calamities into the world, including patriarchy (Genesis 3:16), death (Genesis 3:19), and even animal exploitation (Genesis 3:21). This current world filled with misery, carnivory, sickness, disorder, difficulty, and mortality was never God's intention.

However, all is not lost as God promises the New Earth when Jesus returns. This is essentially a restored Eden (Isaiah 51:3), where death (Isaiah 25:8), disease (Isaiah 35:5–6), and even animal exploitation (Hosea 2:18) will no longer exist. The Bible is clear that there will be animals on this eternal New Earth (sometimes synonymous with heaven). This book derives its title from Hosea 2:18, which is just one of the many Old Testament verses (including Isaiah 11:6–9 and 65:25) prophesying a future eternal peace between humans and animals when Jesus returns to inaugurate the New Earth. Micah 4:8 confirms this Edenic dominion being restored. There are passages in the New Testament mentioning the New Earth as a place of justice (2 Peter 3:13) with no death, mourning, crying, or pain forevermore (Revelation 21:4).

The Christian Animal Rights Association acknowledges biblical personhood and this future peace and harmony God intended all along. We are guided by the Lord's Prayer, which Jesus taught us in Matthew 6:10, in which he stated, "Your kingdom come, your will be done, on earth as it is in heaven." We strive to live with the same sense of justice on earth as is in heaven. Exploiting animals is not ideal, as it did not happen in Eden, nor will it happen on the New Earth. Thus, we should try and make that a reality here and now, as well. The logical implication of these beliefs is the abolition of the property status and exploitation of animals.

How can we help humans and animals to live in harmony here and now on this earth and therefore reflect God's ultimate will? How can we help achieve the peace and harmony God desires for his sentient creations? I have developed an approach called New Earth Abolition (NEA), that can help achieve God's ideal here and now. This concept combines the peace and harmony we see in Eden and the New Earth and the teachings of Jesus in order to help free creation from its current oppressive human bondage and exploitation. NEA is discussed in the next chapter.

4

New Earth Abolition (NEA)

Secular Abolition

MERRIAM-WEBSTER DICTIONARY DEFINES ABOLITION as the act of officially ending or stopping something: the act of abolishing something.[1] Welfarists seek to continue to exploit animals in a kinder way. In contrast, abolitionists seek to end animal exploitation altogether. Gary L. Francione is a well-known secular animal rights abolitionist. On his website, Animal Rights: The Abolitionist Approach, Francione states, "Right now, the discussion about animals is focused on treatment and how to 'improve' animal exploitation. As of this time, there really isn't any serious discussion about whether we should use animals at all. So let's work toward changing the conversation from treatment to use; from welfare to abolition; from 'happy exploitation' to no exploitation."[2] Francione, like nearly all animal rights activists, is unwittingly operating by scriptural principles, as his beliefs match the biblical ideal. Thus, the Christian animal rights objective should be abolition, which is the end of animal exploitation. Animals are, in fact, persons, and

---

1. Merriam-Webster.com Dictionary, "abolition," definition 1
2. Francione, "Quotes."

New Earth Abolition (NEA)

therefore we must cease to harmfully exploit them. This cessation can be accomplished by applying the principles of NEA.

The Three Tenets of NEA

These are three requirements for NEA to work. First, we show equality where applicable to animals. Second, we should serve the animals as an ideal. Finally, we are to try our very best to live in harmony with animals. This approach will help reflect God's ideal and intent for all of creation seen in Eden and the prophecies about the New Earth.

1. Humans treat animals the way humans would want to be treated themselves.
    a. The Golden Rule (Matthew 7:12, Luke 6:31)
    b. The Second Great Commandment (Matthew 22:39, Mark 12:31, Luke 10:27)
2. Humans serve animals, they do not exploit them. (Mark: 9:35, Philippians 2:3–4)
3. Humans foster harmony with and between animals. (Genesis 1:20–30; Isaiah 11:6–9, 65:25).

In summary, humans should treat animals with:

1. Equality
2. Servanthood
3. Harmony

With these concepts in place, Christians can put this into action by looking at all the ways we exploit animals and determine if they align with the principles of NEA. How humans exploit animals is endless. However, I focus here on the four most common harmful ways humans exploit animals, which obviously do not align with the principles of NEA. All four of these exploitative industries use and abuse animals instead of treating them with equality and servanthood. These industries also cause strife and disharmony between species.

A list of resources is provided at the end of the book. Examining and finding alternatives to this exploitation is the first step toward humans living as harmonious equals and servants to animals.

Animals Exploited for Food

Farm animals are frequently dehorned, castrated, crammed into tiny cages, and denied any sort of ethical consideration (like anesthetics) within the heavily industrialized agriculture of the modern world. These animals raised for food live short, painful lives that usually end in agonizing and horrific ways. Most of humanity cannot handle the footage that is captured from this process. Fortunately, the Bible offers a solution.

As stated previously, God's original and ideal intention was the veganism we see in Eden (Genesis 1:29–30). The New Earth will return to God's ideal of veganism as well (Isaiah 11:6–9; 65:25; Hosea 2:18). Thus, by applying the principles of NEA, the Christian Animal Rights Association advocates informed veganism as a way to actively live out the Lord's Prayer (Matthew 6:10). Our ministry advocates against the consumption of meat and all other animal products such as dairy, eggs, and even honey. By ceasing to consume animal products, Christians treat animals the way Christians would want to be treated. Lactating human mothers, for example, would not want their babies taken, cramped in a stall, and eventually turned into veal, which is what happens to cows and their calves, respectively. Imagine yourself as nearly every farm animal in America, whose death has already been determined based on the consumer market. None of us would want to be treated like that.

The Bible not only explicitly endorses veganism as God's ideal in Genesis but also in discussing the diet of the prophet Daniel, which was described in Daniel 1:1–21. The chapter describes Daniel as he was taken to Babylon to serve King Nebuchadnezzar

New Earth Abolition (NEA)

and learn the language. Daniel requested and consumed only vegetables and water instead of the king's food. After ten days, Daniel appeared to be in better health than his peers who ingested the king's cuisine. A 2010 study showed participant decreases in blood pressure and cholesterol, confirming the health benefits of Daniel's Diet.[3] Daniel was vegan long before the word was coined by Donald Watson in 1944!

Christians often think vegans eat nothing more than twigs and berries. However, this is because most concentrate on what they have to lose rather than on what they have to gain. In my experience, in the standard American diet, all meals revolve around the meat portion, which often limits meal creativity. Veganism sparks creativity as it instead can educate you on the 200,000+ species of edible vegetation[4] that God has bountifully given us for food, which are usually ignored in the standard American diet.

It is common knowledge that consuming plentiful and varied fruits and vegetables is healthy for the human body. In fact, a 2020 analysis of 16 studies determined vegan diets can promote weight loss and can decrease body mass index (BMI), LDL, and total cholesterol. Veganism can assist in controlling blood sugar, and decrease arthritis symptoms.[5] Indeed, this mountain of evidence can be confirmed by the Academy of Nutrition and Dietetics' statement about veganism. The organization declares informed veganism and vegetarianism as healthy, nutritionally sufficient, suitable for every phase of the lifespan, capable of averting common chronic illnesses, and may even be helpful in healing some diseases. The Academy also touts these regimens as being better for the environment than heavy animal product-derived diets. However, they caution the need for vegans to have a dependable vitamin B-12 source.[6]

From a Christian perspective, these health, environmental, and animal-related benefits of veganism can easily be explained.

3. Bloomer et al., "21 Day Daniel Fast."
4. Gammill, "200,000 Species Edible Plants."
5. Petre, "16 Studies on Vegan Diets."
6. Melina et al., "Position of the Academy," 1970–1980

This is the diet God always desired for humanity. That is the best part about veganism for Christians. It not only benefits health, stewardship of the planet, and animals, but it is a way for Christians to live in accordance with God's values. Many Christians shudder at the abuse rampant in modern industrial agriculture. Veganism is important because it allows Christians to cease from harming and exploiting animals, and instead, treat them with harmony, equality, and servanthood. Veganism is a way an individual can prepare for, and experience one small part of the future New Earth God has in store for us!

Animals Exploited for Experimentation

The garden of Eden story found in Genesis indicates that humans and animals lived harmoniously without any sort of exploitation. Experimentation on animals is particularly brutal. Undercover footage often shows animals shoved into filthy cages, with infected incisions, and instruments protruding from their orifices. Using Jesus' principle of equality, it is safe to say no human would want to experience that. Human experimentation also has a sordid and painful history. Per the application of NEA, the Christian Animal Rights Association seeks to abolish experimentation on animals. Instead, our ministry advocates cruelty-free products. There are many companies in this consumerist age that circumvent their products from being tested on animals. Cruelty-free products are important because they give humans the opportunity to treat animals with harmony, equality, and servanthood. It is important to note that our ministry does allow observational research. A researcher who is observing and gathering data on wild or domesticated animals in a natural setting, and is not disturbing or harming them, is appropriate and does not violate the principles of NEA.

Animals Exploited for Fashion

The fur industry not only changes fast, but has a long and painful record of being cruel toward all sorts of animals. Foxes, mink, chinchillas, and others are often farmed for their fur. Footage often shows them caged and driven to insanity from the confinement. Many wild animals are trapped for their coats, including beavers, wolves, and coyotes. This vicious process causes painful injuries to their limbs before they are killed for a luxury item.

The leather industry is also cruel, but exists primarily as a byproduct of animal agriculture, as most leather comes from cows, pigs, sheep, and other domesticated animals who are first killed for their meat. However, some wild animals like snakes, crocodiles, and alligators are hunted or farmed specifically for their skin to be made into bags and boots.

Using the principles of NEA, the Christian Animal Rights Association promotes ethical fashion alternatives, such as synthetic and plant-derived materials, which contain none of the cruel processes that fur and leather do. These cruelty-free fashion materials are important because they allow humans to treat animals how we would want to be treated and give humans the chance to live as harmonious servants to the animals.

Animals Exploited for Entertainment

Circuses train animals to perform dangerous tricks and stunts. The training generally requires harm. Animals do not just jump through flaming hoops without some fear of being beaten for not doing so. Other uses of animals in entertainment, such as dog and horse racing, rodeos, bullfighting, and cockfighting, require harmful animal exploitation.

Zoos and aquariums are often non-profit organizations. I think these facilities have a noble idea, but even the best are not able to properly care for wild animals. It is harmful to keep an animal confined to an environment that frustrates their desire for freedom. The main problem with these facilities is that they are geared toward entertaining humans, not caring for animals.

By utilizing the principles of NEA, the Christian Animal Rights Association advocates for human entertainment that does not involve harming animals. There are many circuses and sporting events featuring willing human participants. These activities allow humans to apply equality and servanthood to animals, which can help sow the seeds of harmony between species.

Wild Animals

As one can imagine, surviving in the wild is incredibly difficult. Animals must constantly face the threats of deprivation, predators, and inclement weather. To add to this already-challenging existence, animals must navigate the difficulties humans place in their way, as well, such as speeding cars on highways, new land development, and the callous recreations of hunting and fishing, to name but a few. As of this writing, wildlife is being decimated at a staggering rate. By approximately 2100, scientists predict half of all species will be forced to contend with extinction. Due to human activity, our planet is losing biodiversity at an astronomic rate.[7] With what little wildlife we have left, it would probably be best if Christians left them alone. We can wait for Jesus to return to fix carnivorous and omnivorous behavior in the wild. Still, we can offer ways for wild animals to function without the fear of harmful human activity. For instance, humans could build wildlife bridges over significant highways to protect the countless animals hit by moving vehicles every year. Humans could stop demolishing what small amount of woodlands remain and perhaps fence off those areas. The development of those lands forces animals out onto highways and into human neighborhoods. These methods would allow humans to equally consider the wild animals affected by our actions. The wild is incredibly difficult at times, and giving animals

---

7. McKie, "50% of Species Extinction."

equal consideration and serving them with our actions would allow for a more harmonious relationship.

Most of all, humans need to cease hunting. We hear all the time about how humans need to control the population of individual animals like deer. Hosea 2:18 states explicitly, *I will abolish the bow*. As we see on the New Earth, hunting will no longer exist. Part of serving animals means realizing we cannot just kill them whenever we would like to. Just like none of us would like to be riddled with bullets, so too we should give animals that equal consideration. Wild animal populations should be dealt with harmoniously. Hunting, therefore, should be a last resort. Only when all other options have been exhausted should hunting even remotely be considered. Other methods, such as immunocontraceptive (birth control) darts or catch-neuter/spay-release, should be employed instead. These same principles should apply to fishing, as well, which is primarily done for recreation, much more than to meet any nutritional need.

The Question of Self-Defense

The vast majority of humans in contemporary industrial cultures can live without harming animals. However, there are a few exceptions. For instance, in any situation in which a human's life is immediately threatened, it is acceptable to kill animals out of self-defense or in order to survive. This principle is also applicable when dealing with other humans (Nehemiah 4:18). For most humans in modern society, however, this should not be a problem. They can meet their needs for food, household products, keeping warm, and entertainment in other ways.

You may be thinking: If humans are no longer exploiting domesticated animals, how will these creatures continue to exist? Our next chapter examines how our ministry approaches this question of future domestication.

5

The Fate of Domesticated Animals

THE VAST MAJORITY OF humanity recoils at animal slaughterhouse footage. The reason is evident in the light of Christianity, which shows that animals were originally designed to be friends, not food, to humanity in Eden. God understands the care and concern we feel for animals. It was God who designed it that way when he told Adam to name (Genesis 2:19–20) and care for the animals (Genesis 1:26). I used to think Adam named the animals by species, but the biblical principle of naming is far more meaningful. Naming indicates a special relationship, much like God named (really, renamed) Abram to Abraham in Genesis 17:5, renamed Sarai to Sarah in 17:15, and renamed Jacob to Israel in 32:28. Jesus also renamed Simon to Peter in John 1:42. Similarly, humans all over the world share their homes with companion animals and give them names. For instance, we rescued a husky in 2015 named Roxy, but we instead dubbed her Zira. This human-companion animal friendship is a living embodiment of God's original, ideal intention for dominion. Though in our experience, Christian clergy and believers will often scoff at human and animal bonds as merely saccharine or childish. However, the Bible indicates this is not mere sentimentality as all animals were intended to be companions in Eden. The human and animal friendship is as legitimate as any other, from a biblical standpoint. Domesticated animals, though, present a problem in traditional animal rights philosophy.

The Abolitionist Approach and Domestication

A thorny issue involved within animal rights philosophy is the question of the ultimate fate of domesticated animals. Animal rights abolitionist pioneer Gary L. Francione was interviewed on *The 180* of the Canadian Broadcasting Corporation (CBC) Radio, stating, "I'm arguing that we ought to get rid of domestication altogether." He of course advocates caring for domesticated animals alive currently, however.[1] I partially disagree with his stance of phasing out domestication.

Domestication Stance as Critical Fodder

I do not want it to appear that I dislike or find contempt with any of Francione's approach. I think his abolitionist stance is the best secular version of animal rights. I can only assume, but I think Francione and many other animal rights activists and groups advocate extinction because it is easier to approach domestication that way. As the previous paragraph shows, domestication is a sticky issue that is hard to navigate. Advocating extinction sweeps the whole issue under the rug, seemingly in an attempt to avoid talking about it. However, I believe the desire to eliminate companion animals and domestication altogether is a hindrance to animal rights overall. For instance, that same CBC interview print headline reads, "Believe in animal rights? Be prepared to go pet-free." This title is of course meant to cause a reaction, but I do think many humans are turned off by the concept of animal rights because it seeks to end the domestication of animals. I think animal rights may lose a substantial percentage of individuals who would join the movement, but are worried they would be condoning the extinction of domesticated companion animals. Advocating

---

1. Francione, "Believe in Animal Rights?"

extinction of domesticated animals creates easy fodder for the enemy to throw against animal rights activists, soiling the obvious moral high ground of the animal rights movement. Some have leveled criticism against Francione for his statements. For instance, Wesley J. Smith wrote a 2016 article titled, "Animal Rights Means No Dogs and Cats", which was published by the *National Review*. Smith criticizes Francione's stance throughout and ends the article by stating, "Boiled down to its essence and beneath the sentimentality, the animal rights movement is anti-human."[2]

Presuppositions

In order to address my disagreement with Francione over domestication, we must first address our presuppositions. Francione seems to operate from a naturalistic and evolutionary worldview. For instance, an article he wrote titled "Our hypocrisy" was featured in a 2005 publication of *New Scientist*. He states, "It is astonishing that 150 years after Darwin, we are still so surprised that other animals may have some of the characteristics thought to be uniquely human. The proposition that humans have mental characteristics wholly absent in non-humans is inconsistent with the theory of evolution."[3] I'm speculating, but I imagine working from an evolutionary perspective on animal rights would see domestication as ultimately bad as it took animals from the wild and made them subservient to and dependent on humans.

As stated previously, I am not operating from an evolutionary perspective, but rather arguing for abolition based on what God intended the human–animal relationship to be all along, as recorded in Genesis 1:20–30. In Genesis 1:25, the text specifically mentions God creating separate categories of animals, first the wild animals and then the livestock. The context indicates that the livestock were not intended to be eaten, but rather that they were always supposed to have a close, friendly relationship with

---

2. Smith, "Animal Rights Means No Dogs and Cats."
3. Francione, "Our Hypocrisy," 51.

The Fate of Domesticated Animals

humans. Thus, domestication is not seen as bad, but rather as God called it at the end of Genesis 1:25: good. That is the critical difference between Francione's Abolitionist Approach and NEA. Where the Abolitionist Approach sees domestication as problematic, NEA sees human exploitation by abusing the divine command of dominion over animals as the problem. Utilizing the principles of NEA, the Christian Animal Rights Association seeks to instead reform domestication, not abolish it.

For clarity's sake, it was not until Genesis 9:2 in this fallen world, after the flood and Noah's ark, that all animals, except livestock, started to fear and dread humans. In context, this was clearly not ideal. However, we see God's ideal intention of domestication again in Isaiah 11:6 and 65:25, which sees wild animals, such as wolves, peacefully intermingling with livestock animals, such as lambs. Although the New Earth verses (Isaiah 11:6–9, Isaiah 65:25, Hosea 2:18) will most likely require divine intervention to be fully accomplished between wild animals, we can still foster peaceful harmony between humans and domesticated animals. The New Earth gives us further evidence that harmful exploitation and abusive interpretations of dominion are the primary problems requiring correction, not necessarily domestication.

NEA and Companion Animals

Dogs and cats are the primary companion animals in the United States. The way these animals are bred for profit does not line up with the personhood rights for which the Christian Animal Rights Association advocates, as breeding and selling treats them like property. Nevertheless, companion animals in our world are a microcosm of the ideal God had for humans and animals in Eden. Our ministry advocates that companion animals be treated how most Americans already behave towards them, with equality and servanthood. Companion animals are generally considered members of the family and are valued for who they are, not for the commodities they provide to humans.

Unfortunately, by law, companion animals are treated as property, but this is something the Christian Animal Rights Association seeks to change with personhood laws. The concept of companion animals is not inherently a bad one, but in practice, it could be improved. According to recent statistics, an estimated 860,000 cats and 670,000 dogs are euthanized yearly in United States animal shelters,[4] which is inexcusable. Thus, the Christian Animal Rights Association advocates adopting companion animals from shelters and rescues, rather than buying bred companion animals, who are often from puppy mills. Our ministry stands firmly against the practice of buying and selling animals and the humans who make a profit from this breeding business.

Another important portion of NEA is not only fostering harmony between humans and animals, but between other species as well. For instance, most humans feed the dogs in their care meat. It does not make any sense to feed dogs the bodies of another species. The Christian Animal Rights Association advocates feeding dogs informed vegan diets. I expect much criticism over this, because a stigma exists around feeding dogs non-carnivorous diets. The almost exclusive argument is: Don't force your opinions on dogs. However, this is easily refuted by hypocrisy, as the claimer is forcing other species to die because of their opinion about dogs. Significant scientific literature exists declaring that feeding dogs vegan diets is safe, and has health benefits.[5] It makes sense, as dogs have existed alongside humans for thousands of years, eating scraps. Resources for vegan dog food are available at the back of the book.

It becomes tricky with cats however, as they are obligate carnivores. There are vegan cat food brands that contain synthetic substances found in meat. In our experience, some cats tolerate it, others not so much. However, as a last-resort, meat can be justified for cats, as they require it, whereas humans do not. A better alternative to vegan cat food would be the burgeoning product known as lab-grown meat. This high-tech creation will hopefully be on

---

4. ASPCA, "Pet Statistics."
5. V-dog, "Vegan Diets for Dogs."

shelves soon. Lab-grown meat is growth of a biopsy of flesh in a petri-dish, or bioreactor, simulating the way the body typically creates muscle. Theoretically, this is a slaughter-free meat that would be perfect for companion animals who are obligate carnivores.

NEA can be seen as a middle-ground between Francione's Abolitionist Approach and the much softer animal welfare paradigm. NEA sees animals as persons who are no longer property but still sees domestication as valuable, as evidently, God does. I think the biblical understanding of animal rights is actually a much nobler pursuit. Francione's advocacy of domestication extinction, in my opinion, and biblically, would not be true justice. Biblical justice would not just be letting our victims become extinct, but rather forging a new relationship, one built out of service and harmony rather than exploitation and death. One pivotal way the Christian Animal Rights Association seeks to forge a new relationship is by changing the way we talk about animals.

Changing Our Language

Humans tend to approach the world from our point of view, which is known as anthropocentrism. This is a major reason why many Christians think everything, including animals, was created for human use and benefit. On the contrary, the Bible makes it clear that God created everything for himself (Psalm 104:24, Colossians 1:16). Despite thousands of years of Christian dogma being used to exploit animals, it is essential to remember that humans do not ultimately own animals. God owns them. Psalm 50:10–11 states, "For every beast of the forest is mine, the cattle on a thousand hills. I know all the birds of the hills, and all that moves in the field is mine." Therefore, we need to approach the world from a theocentric perspective, or as God would view it.

I am no fan of political correctness, but I bring these verses into the discussion because I think our language needs to change. For instance, in our culture, we often say we "own" dogs and cats. We may own them legally (which the Christian Animal Rights Association seeks to change), but we should not say those words. We are their "caretakers," "guardians," or even "parents." Our culture sometimes calls animals "it" within a sentence when we should be saying, "him," or "her." If the sex of the animal is unknown, perhaps, "them." I know this sounds silly at first, but think about it: Would we ever refer to any human as "it?" We see this inconsistency in biblical translation. For instance, Isaiah 34:15 uses "her" to describe owls, but Matthew 12:11 uses "it" to describe sheep. One way to acknowledge animal personhood would be to consistently use personalized pronouns that reflect who animals are—someone, not something.

The same goes for many of the idioms we use without even thinking about it. For instance, many humans casually say, "We can kill two birds with one stone", or "We have bigger fish to fry." Although they do not directly hurt animals, our language has a way of informing the way we think. Our ministry seeks to reform language in this way, as few would think it acceptable if we said, "We can kill two kids with one stone", or "We have older grandmas to run over." Society values humans and is repulsed by violence (as it should be). We should treat animals the same way by not using them in violent idioms. We can easily replace these terms with nonviolent ones, such as, "We can cut two potatoes with one knife", or "We have bigger zucchinis to fry." Best of all, the idioms still work this way and do not lose their intended meaning.

Caring for animals who need homes and changing our language are but two things we can do to help animals now and build a better world for them in the future. I also intend to discuss what the world may look like in the future if the world were to follow the principles of NEA.

A Possible Future for Domesticated Animals

The other social issue where abolition was pursued was human slavery. Although a war was fought to end it in the United States, the end goal was fairly straight forward in that slaves would stop being property and could simply be free and assimilate into society. This was clouded by racism and other issues but these slaves,

The Fate of Domesticated Animals

once freed, at least had the inherent ability to participate in society like their free human peers. The abolition of animals is more complicated, as the animals obviously do not need to integrate into human society, but rather they desire to be left alone and be free from harm and exploitation. The question then becomes: What shall we do with domesticated animals once we achieve liberation?

I personally have heard arguments from meat-eaters stating that they eat animals because, without human demand, the animals would have never existed. I do not think commodification is a justifiable reason to bring someone into the world. However, it does bring up an interesting question about what will happen to domesticated animals if and when humans stop breeding them to keep up with market demand. This question is many, many decades, and perhaps even centuries from ever needing to be answered. The question of what will happen to domesticated animals only rests on the planet adopting worldwide veganism, finding alternatives to exploiting animals, or a combination of both. The Christian Animal Rights Association hopes that as more humans integrate these compassionate options, fewer and fewer animals will be brought into the world to keep up with the demand. None of the rest of this chapter includes any particular plan that the Christian Animal Rights Association endorses, but is rather mere speculation and an attempt to forge a hopeful future for domesticated animals.

I do agree with Francione when it comes to extinction, although only about certain breeds of domesticated animals. For instance, non-wild turkeys have become so genetically altered, they cannot copulate and reproduce without human intervention.[6] Similarly, domesticated chickens have been bred to grow much larger than their ancestors. This chromosomal tinkering has caused these birds to suffer from joint ailments and persistent discomfort regardless of the nightmare they are forced to endure from modern animal agriculture.[7] If I were one of these animals, I would prefer extinction to a drastically unnatural and painful life.

6. Taylor, "Humans Have Changed Turkeys."
7. Piper, "Chickens in Constant Pain."

Based on the principles of NEA, I would rather not exist than have the debilitations domesticated turkeys and chickens suffer from as they develop.

However, some domesticated animals can still breed and have happy and healthy lives in a proper setting. One thought would be to introduce them to the wild. However, this is not a practical solution concerning individual domesticated animal well-being, as they tend to face a high probability of death in this situation.[8] Thus, I do not support this. My thoughts have led me to two different approaches, one being the ideal and the other being more realistic.

The Ideal Approach

The ideal approach activists could consider on behalf of domesticated animals is one of reparation and restitution to them. I believe strongly in this concept, not only as an act of justice, but because it is a concept we see modeled in Jesus' interaction with the tax-collector Zacchaeus (Luke 19:8). Animals have often been exploited in the past because it may have been necessary for survival. However, in recent times, society has unjustifiably exploited animals for reasons such as pleasure, culture, and convenience.

Perhaps our future society could allow domesticated animal protection on federal ground. The U.S. paid reparations to Japanese-Americans who were unjustly harmed and incarcerated during World War II. Many other human groups are still waiting on their deserved reparations. The United States and perhaps the rest of the world needs to at least start discussing the possibilities of reparations to domesticated animals in the future. After killing billions of animals every year globally times however many years this continues, it is the least humans can do for them. A federal farm sanctuary that manages a small fraction of domesticated animals who exist today does not seem to be outside the realm of possibility. This theoretical sanctuary would be a reparation to

---

8. Barber, "Domestic Animals in the Wild."

domesticated animals for the unjust treatment and cruelty humans have inflicted on them. The animals would ideally be protected by personhood laws, preventing them from being exploited in any way. Their existence would not be valued based on what they can do for humans, but rather they could live in this theoretical sanctuary, free to graze and enjoy life as God always intended. Most farm animals can live vegan, as well, which would not require the death of other animals to feed them. This theoretical sanctuary could be applied to any species, even wildlife.

The Realistic Approach

In the future, if and when domesticated animals are no longer brought into the world for exploitation by humans, their existence could continue on in the forms that they already do, as seen at non-profit animal sanctuaries. There are many farm animal sanctuaries that have popped up all over the country in the last 30 years. These facilities take in farm animals who escaped slaughter, fell off slaughter trucks, or were rescued by animal rights groups. The animals are free to roam the gated facility, where they are no longer exploited for what they can provide. Instead, human caretakers act as servants to the animals by making sure all of their basic needs are met. The best part is, the animals are never expected to give anything back in return. Most Christian animal rights activists would agree that this beautiful situation is exactly what was intended in Eden all along. However, as of right now, the vast majority of these sanctuaries do not allow the animals to breed because space is needed for future escaped or rescued animals who may need a home. The animals at sanctuaries in the future could perhaps breed (if they so desire), raise their offspring without threats of danger, and have their well-being looked after by humans.

This sanctuary idea could be discussed within the concept of other domesticated species, as well, not just farm animals. Instead of dogs having to live in cramped apartments, waiting for their guardians to come home from work, perhaps they could live at a sanctuary amongst their biological parents, siblings, and other dogs. That way, they could be surrounded by their kind and humans could care for their needs, like healthcare. This could be a better way to transform the current companion animal paradigm.

As said previously, it will take many, many generations for this to even require a discussion. Until then, our ministry advocates treating animals with equality and servanthood, and always seeking to live harmoniously with the animals that are here now. The future fate of domesticated animals under human guidance remains a giant question, but our supporters can be assured that the Christian Animal Rights Association will always strive to advocate for the animals' best interests.

6

Addressing Abuse of the Bible

THE THEOLOGIAN ORIGEN, IN his *Fragments on 1 Corinthians*, states, "Men should not sit and listen to a woman . . . even if she says admirable things, or even saintly things, that is of little consequence, since it came from the mouth of a woman."[1] Christianity was embarrassingly comfortable with justifying slavery during the American Civil War. Many prominent Christians cited Scripture to support it. None worse than Confederate president Jefferson Davis, who stated,

> "Let the gentleman go to Revelation to learn the decree of God—let him go to the Bible . . . I said that slavery was sanctioned in the Bible, authorized, regulated, and recognized from Genesis to Revelation . . . Slavery existed then in the earliest ages, and among the chosen people of God; and in Revelation we are told that it shall exist till the end of time shall come. You find it in the Old and New Testaments—in the prophecies, psalms, and the epistles of Paul; you find it recognized—sanctioned everywhere."[2]

Considering these statements above that use the Bible to teach sexist and pro-slavery ideologies, it is clear Christianity, a religion

1. Mowczko, "Misogynistic Quotations."
2. Famous People, "Jefferson Davis Quotes."

founded on the Prince of Peace (Isaiah 9:6), has the potential to be used as a weapon against the marginalized. The common theme in Origen's and Davis's statements is one of serving self rather than serving others.

Serving Others Instead of Serving-Self: Philippians 2:3–4

Many Christians today would agree that both Origen and Davis are violating the principle of Philippians 2:3–4, which states, "Do nothing from selfish ambition or conceit, but in humility count others more significant than yourselves. Let each of you look not only to his own interests, but also to the interests of others." The principle of this verse could beneficially be extrapolated into an interpretive paradigm: we should use the Bible to help serve others and not just serve ourselves. Few Christians today would state that Origen's or Davis's quotes are acceptable. However, those same Christians often use the Bible to justify harming animals to ultimately serve themselves.

Not Taking the Lord's Name in Vain—Exodus 20:7

A similar line of argument as Philippians 2:3–4 is the Old Testament concept of not taking God's name in vain, which is found in Exodus 20:7. It states, "You shall not take the name of the LORD your God in vain, for the LORD will not hold him guiltless who takes his name in vain." This has traditionally been interpreted as not making light of the name of God or using his name in meaningless phrases, which is true. However, a more important understanding of the verse is not using God's name to justify evil and atrocity. Origen's and Davis's invocation of God and his word to justify sexism and slavery, respectively, soils both the faith and the name of God by associating him with obvious scriptural abuse. We see this abuse of the text to justify harming and exploiting animals. Here are a few examples from the web.

Addressing Abuse of the Bible

Weaponizing the Bible Against Animals

In a 2018 *Apologetics Press* article titled "The God-Approved View of Animals", author Eric Lyons, MMin., closes the article with a divine authorization of animal exploitation. He states, "We certainly are to be good stewards of all that God has created, but with animals, this often involves possessing them (Genesis 4:2,4), working them (Exodus 20:10), riding them (Luke 19:34-36), and, yes, even killing them for necessary food and clothing—all of which is graciously permitted by the Creator and Sustainer of life."[3]

There are entire books dedicated to the continued oppression of animals by using the Bible. A July 2019 article by Ann Hess titled "Eating meat should not be question of conscience" was featured in *National Hog Farmer*. Within the article, Hess discusses the book, *What Would Jesus Really Eat? The Biblical Case for Eating Meat*, with co-editor Wes Jamison. He states, "It's a resource for those who attend church or might actually be Christians to defend themselves and also to get the word out. You don't have to be ashamed. In fact, you can rejoice."[4] Not surprisingly, the book was partly sponsored by the Animal Agriculture Alliance.[5]

Our ministry has little doubt that future generations will recoil at statements, like above, that biblically justify harming and exploiting animals, just like most Christians today are appalled by Scripture-based statements that justify sexism and slavery. Using the principle of Philippians 2:3-4, the Christian Animal Rights Association stands firmly against selfishly using the Bible to justify harming others. Instead, our ministry strives to apply the principle of Philippians 2:3-4 by serving and showing compassion toward animals, humbly counting them as more significant than ourselves. Using the principle of Exodus 20:7, our ministry is also careful not to dishonor God's name by justifying atrocities, specifically toward animals. Instead, the Christian Animal Rights Association strives to honor the name of God by showing kindness (Proverbs 11:17) and sympathy (1 Peter 3:8) to all his creatures.

---

3. Lyons, "God-Approved View of Animals."
4. Hess, "Eating Meat Should Not."
5. Bernot, "New Book."

7

Addressing Speciesism

HISTORICALLY, THE BIBLE HAS been used to justify certain grievous forms of discrimination. These harmful teachings have limited the opportunities of individuals and have stood in the way of societal progress. Unfortunately, the church continues to grapple with these issues today, although modern Christians overall seem to be much more aware and open to dialogue about these subjects than they have been in centuries past. The most obvious forms of discrimination the church has and continues to display are sexism and racism.

Historical Sexism

Bishop of Hippo Regius, Saint Augustine, stated, "Woman was merely man's helpmate, a function which pertains to her alone. She is not the image of God but as far as man is concerned, he is by himself the image of God." Christian apologist Tertullian opined, "In pain shall you bring forth children, woman, and you shall turn to your husband and he shall rule over you. And do you not know that you are Eve? God's sentence hangs still over all your sex and His punishment weighs down upon you."[1] Although sexism continues to be a problem within the church, most modern Christian

1. Tarico, "20 Disgustingly Misogynist Quotes."

believers would denounce Saint Augustine's and Tertullian's statements here because they show unjust discrimination based on sex.

Historical Racism

The Bible does not condone racism, but that did not stop some Christians from contriving arguments from it to justify their prejudice. Genesis 9:22–25 explains the curse of Canaan, in which Ham saw his father Noah unclothed. Noah then curses his grandchild Canaan, the son of Ham. Christian racists wrongly justified themselves by distorting this curse to mean black skin, which was absurdly thought to pass on to future generations. Similarly, Genesis 4:15 describes the mark of Cain that was placed on him by God after he murdered his brother Abel (Genesis 4:8). This obscure sign was twisted by racist Christians to mean black skin, a false indication of inferiority.[2] I assume this mark was also thought to be inherited. The vast majority of Christians today would denounce these harmful narratives of both sexism and racism, not just because they are biblical perversions, but also because they show partiality.

Partiality

The issue of discrimination is discussed many times throughout the Bible, and is known as partiality, which Lexico Dictionary defines as unfair bias in favor of one thing or person compared with another; favoritism.[3] A consistent teaching throughout the Bible is one of condemning partiality. This is seen throughout the Old Testament (Leviticus 19:15, Deuteronomy 1:17, 16:19, Proverbs 24:23, and 28:21) and New Testament (1 Timothy 5:21, James 2:1, and 2:9).

God himself is impartial, as mentioned in 2 Chronicles 19:7, Job 34:19, Luke 20:21, Acts 10:34, Romans 2:11, Colossians 3:25,

2. Cline, "Racism in the Bible."
3. Lexico.com, "Partiality," definition 1

and 1 Peter 1:17. Deuteronomy 10:17 in particular states, "For the Lord your God is God of gods and Lord of lords, the great, the mighty, and the awesome God, who is not partial and takes no bribe." Jesus expressed this again in John 7:24, "Do not judge by appearances, but judge with right judgment." The most damning indictment against discrimination is 1 Samuel 16:7, stating, "But the LORD said to Samuel, 'Do not look on his appearance or on the height of his stature, because I have rejected him. For the LORD sees not as man sees: man looks on the outward appearance, but the LORD looks on the heart.'" Discrimination shows partiality to one individual over another and is counter to the principles of God.

Christian Speciesism is Partiality

Despite the obvious biblical denouncement of partiality, one form in particular has been both historically rampant and is barely acknowledged, even today, within modern Christianity. This form is speciesism, which Merriam-Webster Dictionary defines as prejudice or discrimination based on species.[4] This is seen by humans showing favoritism and bias toward their own species and discounting consideration toward other species.

Partiality—The Image of God

The phrase image of God is found in Genesis 1:26–27, and later repeated in Genesis 5:1. All humans, both male and female, are made in the *Imago Dei* (image of God) according to Genesis 1:26–27. This expression is frequently used to justify speciesism. For instance, Kyle Butt, MDiv wrote the 2018 *Apologetics Press* article titled, "Helping Animals is Not the Same as Helping People", concluding, "When God tells us to help the "poor and needy," He is talking about people who are made in His image, not animals."[5]

---

4. Merriam-Webster.com Dictionary, "Speciesism," definition 1
5. Butt, "Helping Animals Not the Same."

This quote, as well as many other popular opinions on what the image of God means, are usually taken widely out of context. In Genesis 1:26, the image of God coincides with the divine order of dominion over the earth and the animals. As previously stated, when paired in context with dominion, our ministry interprets the image of God to mean humans are to mirror the behavior Jesus shows towards those who are under his rule. Christian Animal Rights Association honors this by applying Jesus' principles regarding equality and servanthood, reflected in NEA, to help guide human behavior towards animals. Christian Animal Rights Association believes NEA is emblematic of the divine order to show dominion over animals as image-bearers of God. Thus, the image of God ideally entails humans having responsibility and is not a license to discriminate against animals. Furthermore, the image of God is a characteristic of species membership. Using the image of God to discriminate against animals is partiality because humans and animals are both *nephesh chayyah*.

Genesis 9:6 seems to counter this principle, declaring human life as more important than animal life, based on the image of God. However, in context, Genesis 9:6 occurs right after the flood, a spiritual low point for humanity and certainly not an ideal. Recall that Genesis 6:11 states that before the flood, the earth had become full of violence. I interpret Genesis 9:6 as a temporary dispensation. God had to lower his standard because humanity could not keep his ideal. This is evidenced by God's promise in Genesis 9:11 and 15 never to repeat a flood of extinction-level magnitude again. This means God will not execute his wrath on the entire world again, because his expectations are far less from humanity now. This is also the first time meat is allowed (Genesis 9:3). Importantly, Genesis 9:6 uses the phrase "image of God", but this time, God does not mention dominion like he does in Genesis 1:26. Perhaps the reluctance to using the word is to reflect humanity's spiritual rock bottom, a declaration that humans had now become tyrants rather than good kings.

Furthermore, on Genesis 9:6, since humans could not even be trusted not to kill their own species (Genesis 4:8), placing a higher value on humans in this fallen world (Leviticus 24:17–18; 24:21) could allow humans in the future to realize the importance of animal life too, as seen in Eden and on the New Earth. Andrew Linzey thought similarly about Genesis 9, stating in *Animal Theology*, "Given the corruption of humankind, it was natural and inevitable that moral attention had first to be paid to the regulation of human conduct towards other humans." Earlier he states, "In this respect it is interesting that one highly regarded Talmudic scholar, Abraham Isaac Kook, maintains that the most spiritually satisfying way of reading the practical biblical injunctions concerning killing is in terms of preparation for a new dawn of justice for animals."[6] I thought of an analogy of a family constantly fighting with one another suddenly having the idea of volunteering at a soup kitchen to help impoverished families. Genesis 9:6 is like God advising, "The goal is the soup kitchen, but figure out the differences amongst each other first, and you will be more effective towards other families." Surely the family did not need to have every single issue worked out, but enough so that they could consider helping others.

Humanity was not ready in biblical times. However, even though the headlines may not reflect it, humanity has become more peaceful with each other, as evidenced by the booming population and lack of world war. Though no friend of Christianity, Steven Pinker confirms this notion in his book, *The Better Angels of Our Nature: Why Violence Has Declined*. He states, "Believe it or not—and I know that most people do not—violence has declined over long stretches of time, and today we may be living in the most peaceable era in our species' existence."[7] Based on these observations, we think humanity is ready to embrace the ideal of treating animals as equals, serving them, and no longer using them as resources. Believers are to do their part in helping restore the kingdom by putting Matthew 6:10 into action. Micah 4:8 prophesies Edenic dominion restoration on the New Earth, the perfect display of our status as the image of God. The image of God is an honor that humans should embrace, as the God of the universe

6. Linzey, *Animal Theology*, 131.
7. Pinker, *The Better Angels of Our Nature*, 14.

appointed us as the caretakers of his extraordinary creations, the animals.

Partiality—Cognition

Partiality against animals is shown in other ways too, like cognition. In our experience, Christians will justify speciesism on the grounds that animals are not as intelligent as humans. However, the existence of persons with mental disability, children, and demented elderly humans indicates it is not actually cognition Christians are using to discriminate against animals, but rather just the arbitrary characteristic of species. For instance, University of Cambridge scientists determined that pigs are as intelligent as human children who are three years old.[8] The only reason the human child affords concern is not because of their level of cognition, but rather, only because the human is of our species. The human child is afforded the fundamental rights not to be treated as property and to be free from exploitation, but the pig has absolutely no rights outside of property status. Judging and determining the existence of someone based on their species membership is no different from judging someone based on their race, sex, or mental abilities. Though they are different forms of oppression per se, they all have one overriding theme —partiality. Speciesism is judging someone based on outside instead of internal characteristics. None of us, as far as anyone can tell, controls which body our consciousness is born into. The Christian Animal Rights Association advocates treating all beings who possess *nephesh chayyah* without partiality, which we believe will help restore the kingdom of God.

Why Address Speciesism Now?

The reader may ask themselves how they can address speciesism when sexism, racism, and other forms of prejudice are still so prevalent. Our ministry commonly responds that humanity can

---

8. Newkey-Burden, "You Love Bacon."

always focus on more than one issue at a time. Furthermore, we interpret Genesis 9:6 to be fulfilled based on humanity's growing peacefulness amongst each other. Thus, our ministry believes that racism and sexism may persist because humans have barely begun to address the issue of speciesism. Our ministry believes that focusing on animals first and then humans, will actually help relieve the oppression of both. A 2018 study by Oxford University psychologists was published in the *Journal of Personality and Social Psychology*. The study found that participants who expressed speciesism also expressed human prejudices such as sexism and racism. The authors explained that animal prejudices are linked with human discrimination because they both share the propensity to justify and accept present power structures.[9] We believe speciesism contributes to other forms of discrimination, as today, speciesism is usually the first form of discrimination humans learn. This partiality is first seeded when parents tell their children to love the family dog or cat but eat the cow or pig on their plate. It plants the idea in the child's mind that compassion and love are not universal, but rather, reserved only for a select few. We cannot help but think speciesism contributes to racism and sexism. I have noticed this in my personal experience as well, as it is usually the same humans who see racism and sexism are wrong who realize speciesism also shows unjust partiality. I am not the first to notice this phenomenon. The Greek philosopher Pythagoras famously stated, "As long as man continues to be the ruthless destroyer of lower living beings he will never know health or peace. For as long as men massacre animals, they will kill each other."[10] Renowned author Leo Tolstoy stated the idea more poetically, "As long as there are slaughter houses there will always be battlefields."[11] Thus, our ministry believes that by starting with the most victimized, the animals, we will eventually achieve a better system with less inequality for all. We believe this reflects Jesus' focus on the greatest victims, whom he calls "the least" (Matthew 25:40; 25:45). We will

9. Keim, "Belief in Human Superiority."
10. A-Z Quotes, "Pythagoras Quote."
11. A-Z Quotes, "Leo Tolstoy Quote."

Addressing Speciesism

never accomplish complete fairness and elimination of partiality until Jesus inaugurates the New Earth, but we can strive toward it with the guidance of the Holy Spirit.

Finally, speciesism does not just harm animals, but comes back to harm humans in the end, too. The atrocities humans have committed against animals by the billions have caused mostly untold suffering to humans, as well. For instance, modern animal agriculture is a prominent source of water and air pollution, deforestation, greenhouse gases, and antibiotic resistance.[12] Furthermore, many potentially dangerous infectious diseases such as the swine and avian flu, and possibly even COVID-19, can be traced back to humans exploiting animals for food.[13] The Bible speaks out against this exploitation, as I will discuss in the next chapter.

---

12. Climate Nexus, "Animal Agriculture's Impact."
13. Samuel, "The Meat We Eat."

8

Animal Exploitation: A Biblical Regulation

ANIMAL EXPLOITATION IS SEEN throughout the Bible. Indeed, the multitude of animal sacrifices (Genesis 8:20; Leviticus 1:9), the use of animals for labor (Deuteronomy 22:10; 25:4), and the eating of meat (Luke 24:42–43;1 Corinthians 10:25) is enough to turn any animal rights activist away from the holy text. However, these exploitations and deaths must be seen in the context of biblical regulation, not ideals. For instance, the Pharisees asked Jesus questions about divorce in Mark 10:1–12 and Matthew 19:1–12. Jesus explained in Matthew 19:8, "Because of your hardness of heart Moses allowed you to divorce your wives, but from the beginning it was not so." A hardened heart is a condition which causes humans to rebel against (Hebrews 3:8), distance themselves from (Ephesians 4:18), or ignore (Exodus 9:7) the teachings of God. Jesus is stating that since humanity could not keep the ideals set forth in the garden of Eden (Genesis 2:24), God gave concessions to humanity's limitations in this fallen world. Thus, divorce was permitted but regulated in the Old Testament (Deuteronomy 24:1). In the New Testament, Jesus clarified that divorce was condemned except for a situation like sexual immorality (Matthew 5:32; 19:9). Similarly, a divorce is allowed if a nonbelieving spouse leaves the marriage (1 Corinthians 7:15). However, the ideal would be that divorce never existed. There are other issues which are addressed in the Bible for which recognizing the difference between an ideal and a regulation is critical.

Slavery—A Biblical Regulation

Slavery is an institution that, at first glance, can be interpreted as being endorsed by the Bible. However, biblical slavery was different from transatlantic African slavery to the Americas that took hold from the sixteenth to the nineteenth centuries. Old Testament slavery of Hebrew culture was a means to work off familial debt. New Testament slavery of the Roman Empire was notably different. Slavery in Roman society similarly functioned as a means of debt management in some cases. Although, other slaves may have been born into the institution or became a slave as a prisoner of war. Importantly, Roman slavery was not based on skin color, and in many instances, was only temporary.[1] This context did not prevent some Christians from abusing Scripture, as American slavery was notoriously racist and often a lifetime sentence. A common argument is that transatlantic African slavery was man-stealing or kidnapping, which Exodus 21:16 and 1 Timothy 1:10 condemns. However, a case can be made that most African slaves taken to the Americas were not captured by Europeans. Rather, these slaves were traded by African slave owners in exchange for European firearms. Purchasing slaves from neighboring nations is tolerated in Leviticus 25:44. Once the African slaves were traded and forced into American race-based slavery, they (and frequently their descendants) were often ruled by a ruthless and cruel iron-fist. This was different from the slavery they experienced in Africa, where they typically had legal protection, rights, and kinder owners.[2] Clergy in the U.S. frequently used Scripture to justify slavery. For instance, Baptist preacher Richard Fuller cited Leviticus 25:44 and

---

1. Becker, "Does the Bible Condone Slavery?"
2. Strieker, "Africans' Part in Slavery."

argued that Jesus and Paul did not consider slavery a sin.³ However, slavery must be seen in the context of divorce.

The numerous New Testament passages that discuss slavery (Ephesians 6:5, Colossians 3:22, 1 Timothy 6:1, Titus 2:9, 1 Peter 2:18) can easily be mistaken as an endorsement for the practice. However, several verses indicate slavery was not endorsed, but rather regulated. Slavery is never commanded as an ideal but is rather discussed as an institution with parameters. For instance, Ephesians 6:9 commands masters not to threaten their slaves. Colossians 4:1 commands masters to treat their slaves with justice and fairness. Perhaps most importantly, slaves are not to be considered inherently less than those who are free. Philemon 1:16 recognizes a slave as a beloved brother. Similarly, Galatians 3:28 declares inherent equality between those who are slaves and those who are free. Paul even encourages slaves to gain their freedom and for others not to become slaves in 1 Corinthians 7:21–23. Even in the Old Testament, slavery is regulated by Exodus 21:2, which requires Hebrew slaves to serve six years, and in the seventh are to be set free. Exodus 21:26 demands that a slave be set free if the master injures them.

God's ideal however, would be that slavery never existed, as Genesis 1:26 demonstrates equality and freedom between humans in Eden. On the New Earth, the only talk of slavery we see is in Revelation 22:3. The mentioned servants are not slaves of man, but rather the servants of God. This concept is exemplified in our current world as we, as believers, are slaves of God (Romans 6:22). Just like divorce, slavery was regulated, but it was not an ideal. Slavery arises from man's hardness of heart. This is confirmed when God demanded the Israelites be set free from slavery, but Pharaoh's heart was hard (Exodus 7:13–14, 7:22, 8:15, 8:19, 8:32).

---

3. Menikoff, "Why Did Christians Defend Slavery?"

Animal Flesh—A Biblical Regulation

The killing of animals for food (Genesis 9:3), like human slavery, is an issue that is also not ideal, but is regulated in this fallen world. God's ideal was in the garden of Eden, where humans only ate plants (Genesis 1:29). God gives Noah a reluctant concession to eat animals after the flood in Genesis 9:1–3. This concession was due to the condition of humanity, as before the flood, humans were called wicked and evil (Genesis 6:5). Then after the flood, God called humanity evil again (Genesis 8:21). Furthermore, Genesis 9:4 regulates flesh-eating by demanding that blood not be present when it is consumed.

The context of living in biblical times is essential to discuss. It was probably close to impossible for a human to live without meat or animal products when the Bible was written. It would be a reasonable assumption that meat was necessary for survival in times when plants would not grow, such as during droughts or crop devastation by insects. The Jewish Virtual Library states, "For centuries, agriculture in the Land of Israel was highly dependent on irregular rainfall, making drought and consequent famine of frequent occurrence."[4] This is confirmed within Scripture as well, as famine is described in Genesis 12:10, 26:1, 41:54, 43:1; Ruth 1:1; 2 Samuel 21:1; and 2 Kings 8:1, indicating that it happened often. Drought is described in Jeremiah 14:1–6, with verse 5 stating that there was no grass and verse 6 asserting that there was no vegetation. Joel 1 describes in shocking detail the effects of crop devastation by locusts. Verse 7 describes the destruction of a vine and a fig tree. Verse 10 states, "The fields are destroyed, the ground mourns, because the grain is destroyed, the wine dries up, the oil languishes." Verse 11 describes a ruined wheat and barley field. Finally, verse 12 describes trees that bear no fruit. Lamentations 4:9 gives a description of famine, stating, "Happier were the victims of the sword than the victims of hunger, who wasted away, pierced by lack of the fruits of the field." Verse 10 horrifically describes humans turning to cannibalism, with mothers eating their own

---

4. Jewish Virtual Library, "Agriculture in Israel."

children. During these dark times, human survival would have certainly depended on the flesh of animals. Thus, in Genesis 9:3, meat may have been allowed by God because the earth had previously been flooded, and this had perhaps destroyed most of the plants. The only plant mentioned is that of an olive leaf (Genesis 8:11). Given this context, I postulate that God is stating the meat of animals is acceptable only when one cannot survive solely on vegetation. It is not a license to kill, but rather a permission due to necessity. We are not to eat flesh just because we want to for taste or pleasure. Genesis 9:3 is not an endorsement of slaughter, but rather a permission due to a needful circumstance.

This maxim of necessity is confirmed in another scenario found in the postexilic Tale of the Desert Quail in Numbers 11. In Exodus 16:3–13, God provides quail meat to the starving Israelites. Meat is the last traditional meal before God provides manna in Exodus 16:15. Manna is described in Exodus 16:31, which states, "Now the house of Israel called its name manna. It was like coriander seed, white, and the taste of it was like wafers made with honey." A little over a year later, Numbers 11:4–6 describes the Israelites complaining about the constant manna and their desire to eat other food. God answers their request for animal flesh, ominously stating in Numbers 11:18–20,

> And say to the people, 'Consecrate yourselves for tomorrow, and you shall eat meat, for you have wept in the hearing of the LORD, saying, "Who will give us meat to eat? For it was better for us in Egypt." Therefore the LORD will give you meat, and you shall eat. You shall not eat just one day, or two days, or five days, or ten days, or twenty days, but a whole month, until it comes out at your nostrils and becomes loathsome to you, because you have rejected the LORD who is among you and have wept before him, saying, "Why did we come out of Egypt?"'"

Numbers 11:31–34 then describes a plague from God that struck and killed those who ate the quail meat. God feeding the Israelites quail flesh in Exodus indicates that eating meat out of

Animal Exploitation: A Biblical Regulation

starvation is acceptable in this fallen world. However, to eat meat gluttonously is sinful, as demonstrated by God's action of killing the Israelites who ate quail meat even though they had an unlimited supply of manna. The New Living Translation of Numbers 11:34 specifically calls these meat eaters' tombs the "graves of gluttony." Furthermore, on the concept of meat only for necessity, Proverbs 23:20-21 confirms this notion as the verse condemns the gluttonous eating of meat. My interpretation of Proverbs 23:20-21 is not that it condemns the eating of too much meat, but rather, like Numbers 11:34, that it condemns the eating of meat when we cannot justify it as a meal of last resort. One time this principle would not apply is when God commanded killing and eating the yearly Passover lamb (Exodus 12:14, 12:24), which Christians are no longer bound to due to the sacrifice of Jesus (1 Peter 1:19).

Deuteronomy 12:15, upon first glance, seems to contradict this biblical principle of gluttonous meat-eating. The verse states, "However, you may slaughter and eat meat within any of your towns, as much as you desire, according to the blessing of the LORD your God that he has given you. The unclean and the clean may eat of it, as of the gazelle and as of the deer." This verse functions as a practical amendment to Leviticus 17:3-4, which required slaughtered animals to be brought as a sacrificial offering at the entrance to the portable place of worship, the tabernacle. Deuteronomy 12:15 instead allows slaughter for food away from the tabernacle. The verse is not an endorsement, but rather a regulation. Deuteronomy 12:16 and 12:23 regulates the killing by prohibiting the consumption of the blood.

Blood is seen as a sacred force from God, as it contains life (Leviticus 17:11). The eating of blood is still forbidden in the kosher laws, upheld by practicing Jews even today (Genesis 9:4; Leviticus 7:26; 17:10; 17:14; 19:26; Deuteronomy 15:23; 1 Samuel 14:32-34). The Bible does not give a specific reason as to why ingesting blood was condemned. It would make sense that consuming blood would have been condemned for hygienic purposes, as it is a well-known vector for disease. I think kosher stipulations were a ritualized reminder that slaughter is ultimately the taking of a life and thus a grave matter, not to be taken lightly. Recognizing the shedding of blood would keep the Hebrews from becoming desensitized to killing animals. The laws may have also partially deterred flesh-eating by complicating the process, as fruits and vegetables are kosher. The kosher laws were repealed in the New Testament (Matthew 15:17–18; Mark 7:19; Acts 10:11–15, 11:4–9; Colossians 2:16). Even though Christians are allowed to eat any meat, Proverbs 12:10 condemns cruelty to animals, binding Christians to a standard on flesh-eating concessions. Nearly all meat in modern industrialized countries involves cruelty.

Most importantly, Deuteronomy 12:15 needs to be interpreted in light of Deuteronomy 12:20. This latter verse states, "When the LORD your God enlarges your territory, as he has promised you, and you say, 'I will eat meat,' because you crave meat, you may eat meat whenever you desire." This statement almost seems like God is being facetious! The verse uses the term *crave* to describe the desire for meat. We are reminded of the fate of those who ate the desert quail. Numbers 11:34 states they buried those who had the *craving*. It seems here that God is saying you can eat meat, but there will be consequences if you eat it when you do not need to, such as the desert quail eaters faced in Numbers 11. It is certainly not a blessing. Meat comes with rules and stipulations, whereas an animal-free diet is seen as ideal, as evidenced by God's prescription in Eden (Genesis 1:29). Reverend Andrew Linzey summarizes the regulation of flesh, stating in *Animal Theology*, "The biblical case for vegetarianism does not rest on the view that killing may never be allowable in the eyes of God, rather on the view that killing is always a grave matter. When we have to kill to live we may do so, but when we do not, we should live otherwise."[5]

Animals as Resources—A Biblical Regulation

The Bible seems to be silent on the issue of animal experimentation. However, animal exploitation for resources is discussed

---

5. Linzey, *Animal Theology*, 131

extensively. For instance, leather clothing is mentioned in Genesis 27:16; Exodus 25:5; Leviticus 13:48–49; Numbers 31:20; 2 Kings 1:8; Ezekiel 16:10; Matthew 3:4; Mark 1:6; and Hebrews 11:37. Leather flasks are mentioned in Genesis 21:14; 1 Samuel 16:20; Job 32:19; Matthew 9:17; Mark 2:22; and Luke 5:37–38. Leather tents are mentioned in Exodus 26:14, 36:19, 39:34; and Numbers 4:25. Other leather supplies are described in Exodus 35:7, 35:23; Numbers 4:6, 8, 10–12, and 14. John the Baptist wore camel's hair in Matthew 3:4 and Mark 1:6. The use of goat hair is mentioned in Exodus 25:4; 35:23; and Numbers 31:20. Wool was also common, as evidenced by Leviticus 13:47–48, 52, 59; Deuteronomy 18:4, 22:11; Judges 6:37; 2 Kings 3:4; Proverbs 31:13; Ezekiel 27:18, 34:3; Hosea 2:9; and Hebrews 9:19. Most of these materials were presumably obtained from the animals slaughtered for meat and were probably necessary at the time due to inclement weather. Proverbs 12:10 condemns animal cruelty, regulating the use of animals for resources.

These above instances, however, do not reflect an ideal, as there is no indication that animals were used for resources in the garden of Eden before the fall, nor will they be on the New Earth. The ideal would be for animals to enjoy life with no exploitation. The first exploitation of animals occurs in Genesis 3:21, when Adam and Eve are given skins to wear. Although this does not reflect the ideal as it was soon after the fall (Genesis 3:6) and was probably from a sacrifice to forgive their sin (Hebrews 9:22). Clothing is actually the result of the fall, thus the ideal would actually be nakedness (Genesis 2:25), which may explain why nudist colonies are popular. This book is not here to discuss that! A better option, given the fall, would be for clothing to be made from plant materials, like the fig leaves of Genesis 3:7, which Adam and Eve used when they became ashamed of their nudity. Verses about the current spiritual heaven describe believers dressed in white garments (Revelation 3:5; 4:4) or robes (Revelation 6:11; 7:9). Revelation 22:14 describes New Earth dwellers similarly having these robes. This clothing would not be due to shame, though, as it was in Eden (Romans 10:11). Furthermore, these heavenly robes cannot be made from animals because there is no death or pain on the New Earth (Revelation 21:4). Thus, this idyllic principle of no animal harm for clothing should apply to the use of animals in all industries, including experimentation, today.

The use of animals for entertainment is discussed in Genesis 49:6. The verse speaks of two brothers maiming oxen. The NLT specifically states, "May I never join in their meetings; may I never be a party to their plans. For in their anger they murdered men, and they crippled oxen just for sport." This could definitely apply to bullfighting, which harms the animals for the sole purpose of entertainment. Even in this fallen world, the Bible skips regulation and undoubtedly sees animals being harmed for entertainment as sinful, which would certainly be carried over from Eden and onto the New Earth.

Animal Property—A Biblical Regulation

It is evident throughout the Bible that animals can be considered property for uses such as labor (Deuteronomy 22:10). However, this also does not seem to reflect an ideal, as there is no indication that animals were used for labor in the garden of Eden. Adam had a job to tend the garden (Genesis 2:15). He and Eve were to take care of the animals (Genesis 1:26). However, the animals' only assignment was to eat the plants (Genesis 1:30). I presume otherwise they were free to enjoy life as God intended. Animal use for labor was probably needed to help plow and till the fields, because the ground had become cursed after the fall, making edible plant growth difficult (Genesis 3:17–19).

Nevertheless, Jesus acknowledged that sparrows were being sold, but states that even though they have minimal human monetary value, God never forgets them (Matthew 10:29; Luke 12:6). This implies that animals have value to their Creator regardless of the value humans put on them. Similarly, Jesus addresses the importance of helping animals even on the Sabbath, stating in Luke 14:5, "Which of you, having a son or an ox that has fallen into a well on a Sabbath day, will not immediately pull him out?" Jesus states something similar about sheep in Matthew 12:11. Proverbs 27:23 states, "Know well the condition of your flocks, and give attention to your herds." Again, Proverbs 12:10 shows that we may have animals as property, but we cannot just do whatever we want with them. Ownership is regulated within this fallen world, whether it be of humans (slaves) or animals.

The ideal, as it was in Eden (Genesis 1:20-30), and will be on the New Earth (Isaiah 11:6-9; Isaiah 65:25; Hosea 2:18) would be to live peacefully and harmoniously with the animals, treating them as friends (Genesis 2:19-20), not as property or resources. As previously mentioned, Jesus taught us to pray for the conditions of the just world we see on the New Earth, stating, "Your kingdom come, your will be done, on earth as it is in heaven." (Matthew 6:10). Jesus was obviously upset when he cleansed the temple, deriding monetary corruption (Matthew 21:12-17; Mark 11:15-19, Luke 19:45-48, John 2:13-22). Perhaps he was also acting out the Lord's Prayer when he drove out the sheep and oxen (John 2:15) and overturned the seats of those selling pigeons (Matthew 21:12, Mark 11:15, John 2:16).

Animal exploitation, like divorce and slavery, is the result of humanity's desires and limitations in this fallen world, not how God would ideally have it. The Bible provided regulations as a stepping-stone for the eventual abolition of human slavery. Our ministry believes the biblical regulations of animal exploitation will eventually lead to their abolition, as well. Humans must stop their hardness of heart toward the issues facing animals, or it will be our ruin. Proverbs 28:14 declares, "Blessed is the one who fears the LORD always, but whoever hardens his heart will fall into calamity."

Future generations of Christianity must be careful in how they interpret the Bible. We have met many lapsed Christians who have left the faith because of the self-serving actions of Christians they knew. Christians should strive to be what Jesus called "the light of the world" (Matthew 5:14), which I interpret as Christians being a good example and providing solutions to the many problems of our day. Christian Animal Rights Association is committed to being that light of the world by helping to relieve the oppression of animals. When it comes to social justice issues, such as slavery and animal rights, it is unfortunate that Christians abuse the Bible to justify harming others. The Christian Animal Rights Association lives by a staunch motto: If you do not argue from the Bible out of compassion, then do not argue from it at all. Our next chapter focuses on a very compassionate man. It attempts to answer some common questions you may have about Jesus. These have been compiled from questions our ministry most frequently receives. Feel free to use this material to educate those who justify harming animals with the Bible.

9

Questions about Jesus

Question: Did Jesus Eat Meat?

ANSWER: MANY AUTHORS AND theologians believe Jesus was perhaps a vegetarian, and his teachings about animals were lost as Christianity passed through different cultures. Jesus being concerned for animals makes sense because it reflects his character of love, compassion, and mercy, as can be seen throughout the Gospels. As compelling as this argument may be, and as much as I would also like to declare this, the Bible does not indicate that Jesus was a vegetarian. However, as stated in the previous chapter, being a consistent vegetarian in biblical times was probably extremely challenging, if not close to impossible. The notable exceptions being someone who was wealthy and could afford a steady importation of vegetables (like Daniel who was serving a King in Daniel 1:1–21), or the Israelites living on a constant stream of miraculous manna in the desert in Exodus 16 and Numbers 11. I assume this bread was nutritionally adequate, as Psalm 78:24 calls manna the grain of heaven.

Jesus would have most certainly eaten the annual Passover lamb sacrifice throughout his life, as it was required (Exodus 12:14, 12:24), and he never broke the law (Hebrews 4:15, 1 John

3:5). The text implies that Jesus ate the Passover lamb before his death (Matthew 26:21; Mark 14:18; Luke 22:15). Furthermore, Luke 24:41–43 explicitly states that Jesus ate fish. Many Christians take this verse and declare it an automatic license to eat meat, no matter the circumstance or situation. In context, the primary purpose of this verse is to demonstrate that Jesus rose from the dead in the flesh, proving that he is an actual living, breathing being, not just a spirit. Regardless, Jesus had been dead for several days (Acts 10:40–41) and was probably very hungry. He broke bread before this (Luke 24:30) and maybe ate some. Either way, bread may not have provided key nutrients like omega-3 fatty acids, as fish flesh does. Fish flesh is usually more calorie- and nutrient-dense than bread. I think Jesus ate meat outside of the Passover command because, just like those around him, he required it for nutritional purposes. Jesus fed 5,000 men with five loaves of bread and two fish (Matthew 14:13–21; Mark 6:30–44; Luke 9:10–17; John 6:1–15) for that same reason.

As mentioned previously, living in biblical times was a lot different from how we live today. Food was often harder to find, and far less convenient. Humans ate mostly whole grains, starches, fruits, nuts, and vegetables. Goat and lamb milk and cheese, fish, grape preserves, bee honey, and olive oil were commonly consumed. Hunted and livestock meat were primarily eaten only by the rich. Meat was probably expensive when factoring in the costs of feeding and caring for an animal. Thus, among the poor, slaughtering livestock was reserved primarily for feasts with family. Similarly, eggs, butter, and cow milk were seldom eaten,[1] unlike today. This context of Jesus and his disciples in their location 2,000+ years ago with food scarcity is essential to keep in mind. This is unlike the options most of us have today.

Considering all of the modern conveniences like supermarkets, refrigerators, canning, preservatives, and far easier access to year-round fruits and vegetables, I think the real question is: Would Jesus eat meat if he was here in the flesh today? Based on Proverbs 12:10, I imagine Jesus would weep if he witnessed footage from

---

1. Holy Comforter, "Food Common in Time of Jesus," 1–2

factory farms and all the other cruel ways humans handle animals. The grand majority of meat eaten today in modern industrialized nations is solely for pleasure and taste preference, not because it is necessary, as it was in biblical times. Based on the principle seen in the Tale of the Desert Quail (Numbers 11), we believe that Jesus would not have eaten meat, other than when it was commanded, for the sole reason of pleasure and taste preference. Furthermore, Jesus' death ended the previous meat requirement for Passover. Jesus fulfilled the law, which no longer binds Christians to the obligation of eating Passover lamb (1 Corinthians 5:7). This is one reason John 1:29 calls Jesus the Lamb of God. In fact, this is the primary way he served the animals, which is discussed in a later question.

Question: Did Jesus Not Declare All Foods Clean?

Answer: Jesus stated in Mark 7:18–20, "'Then are you also without understanding? Do you not see that whatever goes into a person from outside cannot defile him, since it enters not his heart but his stomach, and is expelled?' (Thus he declared all foods clean.) And he said, 'What comes out of a person is what defiles him.'" This passage is similar to Matthew 15:16–18. These verses are often used against vegans, quote-mining Jesus with the declaration that Christians can eat whatever they want. However, the explanation of this verse is included in the parentheses by the author, as this verse is simply about Jesus abrogating the Jewish dietary laws. This repeal of kosher laws (Leviticus 11:1–47, Deuteronomy 14:3–21) can be found throughout the New Testament and is made especially evident in Peter's vision in Acts 10:11–15 and later in Acts 11:4–9 in which he is told to rise, kill, and eat. The vision is best understood in light of Jesus' statement about defilement, repealing the kosher laws of the Old Testament. These verses have nothing to do with the ethics of modern meat-eating or how humans should treat animals today.

Romans 14:17 is also commonly utilized by Christians to justify eating meat. The verse states, "For the kingdom of God is not a matter of eating and drinking but of righteousness and peace and joy in the Holy Spirit." This would appear to refute all restrictions on food except that verses 14:14 and 14:20 discuss the kosher dietary laws. Thus Romans 14:17 also applies to Jewish dietary laws, not to the ethics of gluttony or cruelty to animals.

Question: Did Jesus Help His Disciples to Fish?

Answer: In John 21:5-17, Jesus does help his disciples to fish. He even cooks, and serves fish for consumption. These verses, as well as Luke 5:4-9, can easily be understood as Jesus endorsing his disciples being employed in a line of work that kills animals. Remember the context of food scarcity. Based on Numbers 11, Jesus would not have advocated that his apostles kill animals unless it was essential. John 21:15-17 reports Jesus telling Peter three times to care for the lambs and sheep. Jesus is calling Peter away from being a fisherman to a role of pastoral care. Jesus had done this before when he saw Peter and Andrew in Matthew 4:18-19, stating as they fished, "Follow me, and I will make you fishers of men." He said something similar in Luke 5:10 to Simon (Peter). Jesus was aiming for Peter to care for Jesus' human followers, whom he dubs the lambs and sheep. This matches Jesus' description of himself as the Good Shepherd in John 10:11. Jesus described one of the shepherd's duties in the Parable of the Lost Sheep in Matthew 18:12-14 and Luke 15:4-7.

I think the lambs and sheep are also the literal animals. Jesus was not only telling Peter to leave his current career for a religious profession. Jesus also wanted Peter to show concern for animals by fulfilling the role of a Good Shepherd. God is described as a shepherd in Psalm 23. Isaiah 40:11 describes the job description: "He will tend his flock like a shepherd; he will gather the lambs in his arms; he will carry them in his bosom, and gently lead those that are with young." Ezekiel 34:14 describes the role, as well: "I will feed them with good pasture, and on the mountain heights of Israel shall be their grazing land. There they shall lie down in good grazing land, and on rich pasture they shall feed on the mountains of Israel." Conversely, Zechariah 11:16 seems to describe a Bad Shepherd, stating, "For behold, I am raising up in the land a shepherd who does not care for those being destroyed, or seek the young or heal the maimed or nourish the healthy, but devours the flesh of the fat ones, tearing off even their hoofs." Ezekiel 34:3 similarly states, "You eat the fat, you clothe yourselves with the wool, you slaughter the fat ones, but you do not feed the sheep." Jesus was leading Peter away from a life of fishing to one of ministry and concern for animals as a Good Shepherd. Jesus set an example when he stated in John 10:15, "Just as the Father knows me and I know the Father; and I lay down my life for the sheep."

Question: Did Jesus Say to Kill the Fattened Calf?

Answer: This statement is found specifically in Luke 15:23 as part of the Parable of the Prodigal Son in Luke 15:11–32. Parables are similar to what we call allegories today, as they are fictional stories meant to communicate a spiritual or moral truth. Similar to how George Orwell's *Animal Farm* allegorizes the Russian Revolution, or Arthur Miller's *The Crucible* is an allegory for McCarthyism, Jesus often used these simple stories as a way to teach a principle. The Parable of the Prodigal Son attempts to convey the idea of God's forgiveness and grace. The father represents God, and the younger son represents a repentant sinner. The fattened calf represents forgiveness and restoration. The father forgives the son for squandering his wealth and celebrates his return with a celebratory meal of a fattened calf. The slain animal represents forgiveness as Hebrews 9:22 reminds us that, "Indeed, under the law almost everything is purified with blood, and without the shedding of blood there is no forgiveness of sins."

The older brother represents a Pharisee, a group that focused on keeping the law and expected a reward for their behavior. The older brother gets upset because he did not misbehave like the younger brother had, yet he did not even receive a young goat.

The aforementioned ruminant represents any kind of reward. The parable ultimately conveys the blessing God bestows on believers who repent, confess, and receive forgiveness rather than on believers who keep the law solely for glory or reward. The animals in this parable are part of a grander metaphor; the parable does not endorse killing animals.

As discussed, meat-eating was a relatively rare event in biblical times. Even today, the phrase "slaughter the fattened calf" means a special celebration of some type because it is not ordinary. A parable can only take effect if the audience understands it. We believe Jesus is not advocating that animals be killed or be treated as property, but rather communicating a message to an audience who treated animals that way. Jesus is not advocating for killing animals just like he is not advocating for slavery in the Parable of the Unforgiving Servant seen in Matthew 18:25.

Question: Did Jesus Intend for His Teachings to Apply to Animals?

Answer: The most apparent scriptural evidence is when Jesus states, "Do not give dogs what is holy, and do not throw your pearls before pigs, lest they trample them underfoot and turn to attack you." in Matthew 7:6. This could be taken literally, meaning: Do not apply these teachings to animals. Importantly, dogs in biblical times (Psalm 22:16; 22:20) did not have the esteemed status that our culture gives them. They were described as scavengers (Exodus 22:31; 1 Kings 21:23; 2 Kings 9:10; Psalm 59:14–15, 68:23) that lap up blood (1 Kings 22:38) and lick sores (Luke 16:21). Pigs also, just like now, were not respected and were unclean to the Jews (Leviticus 11:7). Psalm 80:13 describes the wild variety as destructive. However, Jesus is using the animals here to make an analogy, warning us to be careful to whom we present the gospel (represented by a pearl in Matthew 13:45–46), as some may not be receptive to it, or may even become violent. Second Peter 2:22 uses similar animal analogies to communicate the idea, stating that believers who know the gospel and turn back are like dogs returning to their vomit and pigs returning to mud after a bath.

There is a question of whether the Golden Rule was intended for animals. The Golden Rule in the ESV translation applies to "others", which is all-encompassing and inclusive. However, some translations use the word "men." This verse presents an odd scenario where translations have a different understanding of who the Golden Rule applies to, so I decided to look at the original text. In the original Greek, the word *anthrōpoi* is used in both Matthew 7:12 and Luke 6:31. *Anthrōpoi*, when translated using Google Translate from Greek to English, is people, which, by my interpretation, would be inclusive of animals. However, *anthropo* is the Greek term for human, as it is the root word for anthropology or the study of humanity, and the root word for anthropomorphize, to give human features. With this understanding, it seems like the proper way to translate Jesus' words would be to say the Golden Rule only applies to humans. This declaration is certainly possible, as, at the time, humans were heavily warring each other, and the thought of peace between even just our species probably seemed like an impossibility, let alone between humans and animals. As stated, animals were needed for food and work at that time in history, so the thought of giving them equal treatment was most likely out of the question. Yet, in some aspects, Jesus implied that humans and animals deserved equal treatment. For instance, in Luke 14:5, Jesus implies that both an ox and a human should be helped out if they fall into a well on the Sabbath.

The Second Great Commandment is a lot more definition consistent, as each verse (Matthew 19:19; Matthew 22:39; Mark 12:31; Luke 10:27; Romans 13:9; Galatians 5:14) uses the term neighbor in almost all of the English translations, all derived from the original Greek *plēsion*, which Google Translate renders as "near", contextually meaning a nearby person. In Luke 10:29, Jesus is asked, "And who is my neighbor?" Jesus responds with the Parable of the Good Samaritan in Luke 10:30–37. This story involves a beaten man on the side of the road. Two Jews ignore the battered man, but a Samaritan shows him sympathy by tending to his wounds and transporting him to safety. In this parable, Jesus is declaring a neighbor as anyone in your vicinity, regardless of any differences. Jesus' use of a Samaritan, a people typically hated by a Jewish audience, indicates this universal application. This story is in continuity with Jesus' other instruction to love your enemies (Matthew 5:44; Luke 6:27). One could argue that the Parable of the Good Samaritan does not apply to animals only because the Samaritan is a human. However, the Samaritan was also a male. Does this perhaps mean the Second Great Commandment only applies to men? Of course not. There is no definitive indication that the Second Great Commandment does not apply to animals, as well.

Paul hints at Jesus' teachings being universal across creation as Philippians 2:4 states, "Let each of you look not only to his own interests, but also to the interests of others." In the original Greek, the word translated as others is *heterōn*, meaning different others. *Hetero* is the etymological root word for heterosexual, or a person attracted to a different sex. It is also the root of heterochromatic or containing different colors. This is an inclusive term that can be applied to all persons of creation.

Even if Jesus' teachings were not at the time directed toward animals, in 2 Corinthians 3:6, Paul teaches that there is a difference between the letter of the law and the Spirit of the law. Following the letter of the law means acting on just what is written. Following the Spirit means understanding and acting on the broad intention of the verse. For instance, Ephesians 5:18 states, "And do not get drunk with wine, for that is debauchery, but be filled with the Spirit." This does not mean that getting drunk with beer or bourbon is acceptable instead! That would be obeying the letter of the law. The Spirit of the law is to avoid being drunk. In light of the Spirit of the law revealed in the Golden Rule and the Second Great Commandment, I think Jesus meant for these verses to be all-inclusive. He intended for people to show concern for one another, regardless of race, ethnicity, creed, sex, social status, and even species. This is supported by Jesus teaching his disciples to be the servants of *all* in Mark 9:35.

We see another animal allegory in the Syrophoenician Woman's Faith in Mark 7:24–30. A parallel in Matthew 15:22–28, states,

> And behold, a Canaanite woman from that region came out and was crying, "Have mercy on me, O Lord, Son of David; my daughter is severely oppressed by a demon." But he did not answer her a word. And his disciples came and begged him, saying, "Send her away, for she is crying out after us." He answered, "I was sent only to the lost sheep of the house of Israel." But she came and knelt before him, saying, "Lord, help me." And he answered, "It is not right to take the children's bread and throw it to the dogs." She said, "Yes, Lord, yet even the dogs eat the crumbs that fall from their masters' table." Then Jesus answered her, "O woman, great is your faith! Be it done for you as you desire." And her daughter was healed instantly.

Jesus' teaching here is allegorical as the dogs represent the gentiles, and the children represent the Jews. The bread is Jesus' mission. Jesus is calling the woman a dog to symbolize that she is a gentile. After the woman states that even dogs eat the crumbs, Jesus responds with the miraculous healing of her daughter. Jesus intended his ministry initially to Jews, but he also intended his disciples and apostles to minister to gentiles later. Paul confirms this in Romans 1:16. However, taken literally, Jesus' miraculous healing indicates that even though children should receive the bread, it is acceptable to share it with the dog. In John 6:48, Jesus stated, "I am the bread of life." Jesus is the personification of the Bible (John 1:1). What are the greatest commandments in the Bible? "You shall love the Lord your God with all your heart and with all your soul and with all your strength and with all your mind, and your neighbor as yourself." (Luke 10:27). Based on the Spirit of the passage, I believe Jesus' explicit use of the children and dog metaphor was him stating his ethical teachings, explicitly the Second Great Commandment, should be primarily applied to humans, but also to animals.

Another verse that our ministry discusses relating to the Spirit of the verse is found in Exodus 20:13, which states one of the Ten Commandments, "You shall not murder." In the KJB, it is famously translated, "Thou shalt not kill." In context, however, this was most likely written exclusively about taking the life of humans. Genesis 9:6 confirms this as well. The multitude of animal sacrifices (Genesis 8:20; Leviticus 1:9) indicates a difference between killing animals and humans in this fallen world. However, we currently live in a time in which animal exploitation can be seen as largely unnecessary in modern industrial nations. Ancient cultures did not have that situation. Thus, using the Spirit of the verse, the Christian Animal Rights Association believes in applying, "Thou shalt not kill" and "You shall not murder" to animals, too. Similarly, many of the verses quoted in chapter seven of this book (which discuss partiality) address human interactions. We also apply the Spirit of those verses to animals.

Question: Did Jesus Ever Consider Himself Equal to or Serve Animals?

Answer: Animal sacrifice is described many times in the Old Testament (Genesis 3:21; Leviticus 4:3). God commanded these sacrifices to deal with human sin (Leviticus 4:14, 4:28). Although, he preferred steadfast love, and the knowledge of God (Hosea 6:6), obedience (1 Samuel 15:22), righteousness, and justice (Proverbs 21:3) more than sacrifices and burnt offerings. Though gruesome, these rituals of slaughter can best be understood as a temporary atonement for sins (Hebrews 9:22).

However, Jesus died on the cross at Calvary as the perfect and final sacrifice (Hebrews 10:1–18). He showed equality with animals as he took their place instead. His sacrifice is another reason why Jesus is called the Lamb of God (John 1:36). Because of Jesus' sacrificial death, animals no longer have to die for human sins. Isaiah 53:7 prophesied about Jesus, comparing him to a lamb led to slaughter. John 10:11 quotes Jesus stating, "I am the good shepherd. The good shepherd lays down his life for the sheep." This verse is commonly understood as symbolic of Jesus atoning for human sin. We believe the verse is also a literal statement of Jesus' service to animals.

Certain premillennial interpretations of the Bible insist that animal sacrifices will return as prophesied by the description of a future restored temple in Ezekiel 40–48, specifically seen in 43:18–27, 44:11, 44:15, 44:23, 44:29–31, 45:15–25, and 46:1–24. Jeremiah 33:18, Isaiah 56:7, and Isaiah 60:7 also show a consistent Old Testament theme of the return of animal sacrifices. However, much of this relies on interpretation. Much of how scholars view Ezekiel's temple depends on how they interpret millennial eschatology, the study of the end times. The presentation of the eschatological views of premillennialism and postmillennialism goes beyond the scope of this book, but I offer a brief contrast. Premillennialism sees Jesus in-the-flesh coming to earth to usher in a literal thousand-year period of social improvement before the Last Judgment; after these events begins the eternal New Earth. Generally, premillennialism relies on a strictly literal interpretation, thus asserting that animal sacrifices will be reinstituted as a memorial. However, this is a seemingly incongruous interpretation method, as Jesus ended animal sacrifices forever (Hebrews 10:18). Other interpretations like amillennialism and postmillennialism more stringently recognize Hebrews 8:13, which declares the new covenant and makes the old obsolete.

I understand the Bible from a postmillennial perspective. This means that I interpret Jesus will return in-the-flesh to establish the New Earth after the millennium (Revelation 20:7), a non-literal prolonged period of social prosperity. Believers are tasked with the Great Commission (Matthew 28:18–20; Mark 16:15–16) to preach the gospel, bringing improvements to all of life. After this millennium, Christ will return to establish the eternal New Earth. Thus, my interpretation of these future animal sacrifices mentioned is that they are symbolic of Jesus' work on the cross. The temple described in Ezekiel 40–48 prophesied Jesus as the temple. Jesus states in John 2:19, "Destroy this temple, and in three days I will raise it up." Jesus is Ezekiel's temple as he was resurrected on the third day (1 Corinthians 15:4). Revelation 21:22 confirms Jesus as the temple, stating, "And I saw no temple in the city, for its temple is the Lord God the Almighty and the Lamb."

Jesus is also the sacrifices. Thus, Ezekiel 43:18–27, 44:11, 44:15, 44:23, 44:29–31, 45:15–25, 46:1–24; Jeremiah 33:18; and Isaiah 60:7 were fulfilled symbolically when Jesus became a perfect sacrifice (Hebrews 10:14). This is further confirmed by Isaiah 56:7, which describes animal sacrifices being conducted on the New Earth. This would seem contradictory as Isaiah 65:25 describes the holy mountain as being a place where there is no harm or destruction. The sacrifices described in Isaiah 56:7 are symbolic of believers presenting their faith in Jesus.

Question: Did Jesus Say that Humans are Worth More than Animals?

Answer: The answer to this question depends on whether Jesus meant that humans would always be more important than animals or if he meant that at that particular time in history, humans were more important than animals. Nevertheless, Matthew 10:31 states, "Fear not, therefore; you are of more value than many sparrows." When discussing anxiety, Jesus states something similar in Matthew 6:26 and Luke 12:24. It is not just birds, either, as Matthew 12:12 quotes Jesus implying that a human is more valuable than a sheep.

However, this is only talking about physical value. Humans and animals are both said to have spiritual value. Ecclesiastes 3:19–21 questions what happens to the spirits of both humans and animals after death. Ecclesiastes 12:7 appears to answer the question. This could be dismissed as the author of Ecclesiastes is probably suffering from depression. However, as mentioned earlier, humans and animals were both given the internal characteristic of *nephesh chayyah* in Eden. This physical and spiritual value difference is expressed regarding other individuals in Scripture too. For instance, 1 Peter 3:7 implies that women are weaker than men, but Galatians 3:28 implies that men and women are spiritually equal. Men are generally physically stronger, yet men and women have equal intrinsic value in God's eyes. What are men to do with this greater physical strength? The earlier context of 1 Peter 3:7 commands a man to show honor to his wife, to not exploit her. Being strong does not give someone the right to exploit someone weaker than them and does not make the stronger person more intrinsically valuable than the weaker one. Similarly, if Jesus meant humans would always be more important than animals, it would be because of physical abilities, not because of anything intrinsic. As mentioned, humans have dominion and were made in the image of God in Eden. However, possessing these two qualities does not afford us the license to abuse animals. Instead, we should act as good kings (Psalm 72:1–17) over them, placing their needs above our own (Mark 9:35). Humans, generally speaking, are more valued for their abilities, but we believe they have the same intrinsic value as animals. Perhaps these analogies may help:

The U.S. president is protected by the Secret Service. Most of us do not have that level of protection. It is not because the president is inherently more valuable than any other human, but rather that the president is more valued because he or she is the leader. It is not that humans are inherently more valuable, but rather that generally, humans can govern animals. Humans are the president, and all other species are the citizens under our rule.

We see this in Scripture, as well, when we look at the ideal conditions of the New Earth and how we will interact with animals then. Isaiah 11:6 describes animals peacefully co-existing and being led by a child. I interpret this child as being symbolic of any believer, as Jesus tells us that we are to become like children to enter the kingdom of heaven/God (Matthew 18:3, 19:14; Mark 10:15; Luke 18:17). We are the divinely appointed leaders of the animals. It is not that they are less important than us, but rather that humans can lead. We should lead domesticated animals and steward wild animals like the good kings God wants us to be.

We also see this in the story of the flood and Noah's ark detailed in Genesis 6 through 9. God specifically told Noah to gather male and female of each kind of animal and bring them into the ark (Genesis 6:19–20). Animals matter just as much to God as humans do, but humans are more valuable because they can take directions, gather the animals, and build the ark (Genesis 6:14–16). A modern example of Noah's ark would be to imagine dominion (Genesis 1:26) as being like a commercial aircraft. God designed the aircraft and has set the destination to the New Earth. Humans are like the pilots, two on-board. This represents male and female humans, made in the image of God (Genesis 1:27). The rest of the craft is filled with passengers (animals), and they have no ability to fly a plane. The pilots and the passengers are both equally valuable to God, but pilots can steer and navigate the plane and are thus more valuable for their abilities. If the pilots get hurt, injured, or die, no one can navigate the plane. Then nobody goes anywhere.

Another possibility is that Jesus could have been emphasizing the importance of human life over animal life due to the time period he was present in, when animals were often needed for food and resources. This reflects a fallen circumstance, as this discrimination was for the purpose of necessity. As mentioned previously, Genesis 9:6 makes a temporary dispensation for humans to value human life over animal life. However, this dispensation was not the ideal and was not intended to last forever, as seen in Eden or the New Earth. Our ministry sees this temporary dispensation in Genesis 9:6 as fulfilled. Like Genesis 9:6, Jesus' statements in Matthew 6:26, 10:31, 12:12, and Luke 12:24 may be fulfilled, given the growing peacefulness humans are showing toward one another in modern times. Thus, believers can do their part in helping to restore the kingdom by putting Matthew 6:10 into action. We can help restore the kingdom by treating animals as equals and serving them, especially since the vast majority of humans no longer need animals as food or resources in order to survive.

With this, I imagine that I will be charged with trying to eliminate human exceptionalism. In reality, I am trying to extend that exceptionalism to others, for it was the attitude of marginalizing outcasts that Jesus actively fought against when he ate with tax collectors (Luke 5:29) and sinners (Matthew 9:11, Mark 2:16).

Questions about Jesus

Question: Did Jesus Drown 2000 Pigs?

Answer: This question is derived from the pericope, The Exorcism of the Gerasene Demoniac, found in Matthew 8:28–34, Mark 5:1–20, and Luke 8:26–39. This admittedly unusual account features Jesus attempting to exorcise multiple demons named Legion from two men. The demons left the men, possessed a herd of swine, then rushed into the sea and drowned. Historically, this tale has been used to justify speciesism. We have a modern example of this with Wayne Jackson's words in the *Christian Courier*. He states, "Anyone who thinks that the value of 2,000 hogs transcends that of a human soul made in the image of God himself (see Matthew 16:26), is so obtuse that likely no argument would be effective in unscrambling the discombobulation within his skull."[2]

Importantly, Jesus did not drown the pigs. In all of the accounts, the demons begged Jesus for permission to possess the herd of swine, and Jesus gave them approval. Presumably, either the demons drove the pigs into the water by force, or perhaps the demons drove the swine to insanity. Regardless, Jesus' actions here may reflect the temporary dispensation of Genesis 9:6, for humans to value human life over animal life. The Christian Animal Rights Association believes Genesis 9:6 has been fulfilled, given the growing peacefulness humans are showing toward one another in modern times. Thus, perhaps Jesus would not have behaved the same way today. Nevertheless, this account may not be literal. I believe this pericope is best understood as a Jewish allegorical political satire, with Legion (a term for a Roman army) representing Roman imperialism and Jesus expelling the oppressive force, returning it to the sea from which it came.[3]

---

2. Jackson, "What about those Gadarene Hogs?"
3. Wilson, "What About the Pigs?"

10

Questions about the Afterlife

Question: Do Animals Go to Heaven?

Answer: Within our ministry, this is a common question. Naturally, believers want to know if they will see their beloved companion animals in heaven. The first thing to discuss is what is meant by heaven. Most people who have been raised in the church know the term, but believe heaven is up in the sky somewhere. There is the current spiritual heaven, which is an alternate dimension where believers in Jesus go when they die (Luke 23:43). Animals are said to inhabit this current spiritual heaven (Revelation 5:13). In the end times when Jesus returns, the souls of believers in the current spiritual heaven will be restored to their everlasting physical bodies on the eternal New Earth (1 Corinthians 15:42), which is sometimes synonymous with heaven. Animals are also found on this eternal New Earth (Isaiah 11:6–9; Isaiah 65:25; Hosea 2:18). However, there is no mention as to whether those are new or restored animals. This begs the question of whether animals have immortal souls.

QUESTIONS ABOUT THE AFTERLIFE

Question: Do Animals have Immortal Souls?

Answer: The Bible is ambiguous on this question. Explicitly, humans have souls (Matthew 25:46), but the Bible does not specifically mention animals having souls. Based on continuity, it is reasonable to assume they do, since new humans are not made in the afterlife. Psalm 36:6 seems to indicate this continuity, stating, "Your righteousness is like the mountains of God; your judgments are like the great deep; man and beast you save, O LORD." This is consistent with Luke 3:6, which declares that all flesh will see God's salvation. I interpret this to mean all types of flesh. Most Christians believe human souls are judged by their acceptance or rejection of Christ's atonement (John 3:16). It is conventionally thought that beings who do not possess the ability to believe or reject Christ, such as children, are saved and given everlasting life (2 Samuel 12:22–23). Other beings, such as animals and cognitively disabled humans, may also be given eternal life, as Psalm 116:6 seems to suggest.

Furthermore, Psalm 49:12–20 poetically implies that material wealth cannot save humanity from death, with verse 20 concluding, "Man in his pomp yet without understanding is like the beasts that perish." Essentially repeating verse 12, this verse implies that humans who rely on their wealth rather than on spiritual insight die like animals. This could, unfortunately, be understood as animals having no eternal life. However, these verses could just be based on the author's visual observations. Other verses that could be indicative of animals not having an immortal soul include 2 Peter 2:12 and Jude 1:10. These verses could also be just observational, as they compare human behavior to animal instinct. These verses do not provide conclusive evidence, as Ecclesiastes also addresses the subject.

Importantly, humans and animals are both said to have spirits as Ecclesiastes 3:21 asks what happens to the spirits of each after death. Ecclesiastes 12:7 answers later that the spirit returns to God, implying that humans and animals both have eternal spirits. Since animals seem to have eternal spirits, it would make sense for them to also possess immortal souls, as these entities are implied to be connected but separable in Hebrews 4:12. Although again, this is not conclusive as Ecclesiastes is ironic throughout. Despite the evidence and ambiguity, Christian scholars and believers often state that animals have no souls or spirits as if this was a logical justification to treat animals terribly. Even if animals do not have immortal souls or eternal spirits, that does not require us to have any less concern for what happens to them. Logically, it means we are to give them more concern, since Christians are to have faith that our joy (Isaiah 51:11) and contentment (Revelation 21:4) will be fulfilled in our afterlife. If this is the only life animals have, then humans should do our utmost to make sure animals are given the absolute best life possible.

Question: Will There Be Meat in Heaven?

Answer: The kingdom of heaven (Matthew 22:2) is a synonym, and is often used interchangeably with the kingdom of God (Luke 14:15). Both phrases primarily indicate the kingdom is spiritually here in the hearts of believers of the church (Luke 17:21). However, the terms can also describe the future New Earth (2 Peter 1:11), where Jesus will reign eternally. The phrases indicate that the kingdom has both started with the church but is not yet finalized. The kingdom will be complete with Jesus' return to the New Earth. This terminology could confuse readers about several passages, which could be misconstrued as meat being present in the eternal state.

The Parable of the Wedding Feast (Matthew 22:1–14) is commonly misunderstood as stating there will be meat on the New Earth. In this parable, Jesus compares the kingdom of heaven to a king who planned a wedding feast for his son. The parable speaks of oxen and calves being slaughtered for the feast. Some invited guests ignore the invitation, and others kill the king's servants. The king retaliates by sending his troops to kill the murderous guests and set fire to their city. The king invites new guests instead. The new guests accept the invitation, but one guest is not wearing the proper attire and is cast out.

The Parable of the Wedding Feast is a larger metaphor with the king representing God the father and the son symbolizing Jesus. The wedding feast itself symbolizes the whole gospel era. The servants are the apostles and evangelists of the early church. The first invited guests are the Jews of Christ's generation. The second set of guests is the gentiles who accept the invitation. Various interpretations exist about why the mis-dressed man was thrown out. Regardless, this parable communicates the eventual accessibility of the gospel to all of humanity regardless of ethnicity or culture, but seems to be particularly criticizing the Jewish multitude of that generation who persisted in denial of Jesus' messianic claims. Importantly, Jesus is not saying animals will be slaughtered for heavenly weddings any more than he is advocating that we kill and set fire to the city of murderous wedding invitees. The kingdom of heaven in the Parable of the Wedding Feast expresses the positive response to the reign of God by believers as they receive the gospel, which will improve the world in many dimensions. The similar Parable of the Great Banquet is found in Luke 14:12–24.

The Lord's Supper description in Luke 22:15–18 can also be misinterpreted as meat in heaven. At first glance, Jesus seems to be talking about the eternal state with Luke 22:16, stating he will not eat the Passover until it is fulfilled in the kingdom of God. It could easily be understood as lamb being served on the New Earth, a reinstitution of the Passover lamb that Jesus was probably eating here. Luke 22:16 is talking about symbolic food, as John 4:34 quotes Jesus stating, "My food is to do the will of him who sent me and to accomplish his work." Luke 22:16 is Jesus essentially stating he will not accomplish the will of God until he dies on the cross and fulfills the Passover. This becomes obvious as Jesus made this the final Passover and instituted the Lord's Supper as a replacement in Luke 22:19–20, as a way to remember his sacrificial death.

Upon first reading, Isaiah 25:6 seems to indicate there will be meat in heaven, served alongside wine. The verse could be referencing the holy mountain of the eternal New Earth. Isaiah 11:9

and 65:25 indicate this holy mountain is a place where all sentient beings will not harm or kill one another. Oddly, some translations (NIV, NLT, BSB, CSB, CEV, HCSB, NET) of Isaiah 25:6 use the word meat (s), which would contradict the New Earth concept of no harm or death as this would require the killing of animals. These seem to be inaccurate translations, as the original Hebrew text does not use the term *bāśār*, which is typically used to indicate meat. The original Hebrew seems to be describing a feast with wine. Regardless, it becomes clear that the feast of food and wine described in Isaiah 25:6 is symbolic of the body and blood, respectively, of Jesus Christ (Luke 22:19–20). The meal symbolizes the sacrifice of Jesus, which secures believers with a home on the New Earth (John 3:16). This becomes clear as Isaiah 25:7 describes a veil that separates all nations from God. Second Corinthians 3:16 states this veil is removed when we believe in Jesus. This symbolic feast imagery found in Isaiah 25:6 describes the marriage supper of the Lamb portrayed in Revelation 19:9, which blesses those invited to the matrimonial dinner to celebrate Jesus and his bride, the church (Ephesians 5:25) in the end-times. Matthew 8:11 details some of the guests that will be seen at this celebration made possible by Jesus' sacrifice, which will include all of his believers.

None of the verses above indicate that humans will eat meat on the New Earth. Meat obviously requires the suffering and death of animals. Thus, meat will not be found on the New Earth, as Revelation 21:4 makes it clear that pain and death no longer exist there. This accords with the vegan world described on the New Earth, where even lions will eat straw like the oxen (Isaiah 11:7, 65:25) and the bears will eat grass (Isaiah 11:7).

Question: Is There Fishing in Heaven?

Answer: Ezekiel 47:10 may indicate this by describing the waters flowing from Ezekiel's temple. Recall that Ezekiel 40–48 was fulfilled by Jesus calling himself this temple in John 2:19. Ezekiel 47:10 states, "Fishermen will stand beside the sea. From Engedi to Eneglaim it will be a place for the spreading of nets. Its fish will be of very many kinds, like the fish of the Great Sea." This verse is symbolically prophetic, with the fishermen representing the disciples and apostles, the nets symbolizing the gospel, and the fish signifying prospective believers. Jesus used a similar allegory in the Parable of the Net in Matthew 13:47-50. This parable similarly states, "Again, the kingdom of heaven is like a net that was thrown into the sea and gathered fish of every kind. When it was full, men drew it ashore and sat down and sorted the good into containers but threw away the bad. So it will be at the end of the age. The angels will come out and separate the evil from the righteous and throw them into the fiery furnace. In that place there will be weeping and gnashing of teeth." Jesus was not advocating fishing. He was allegorizing the Last Judgment (Matthew 25:46).

Ezekiel 47:10 is thought to be about the New Earth because of what is stated two lines later. Ezekiel 47:12 is similar to Revelation 22:2, which describes the New Earth. However, Ezekiel 47:12 is not describing the New Earth, but rather is symbolically describing a believer's relationship to Jesus. Believers are the trees, which receive water from the temple (John 4:14). Believers then produce the fruit of the Holy Spirit (Galatians 5:22-23), which provides spiritual food (John 6:51). These believers also provide healing (Acts 10:38) from the temple himself, Jesus.

Fishing involves an immense amount of pain and eventual death to the fish. Ezekiel 47:10 certainly cannot be about the New Earth because Revelation 21:4 describes the New Earth as a place where there will be no more death or pain. Speciesist believers will attempt to exclude animals from this moral consideration, but Hosea 2:18 confirms: This future eternal covenant of peace and tranquility applies to animals, too.

Question: How Can There Be Fish on the New Earth If There Is No Sea?

Answer: Revelation 21:1 has been interpreted to mean that there will be no bodies of water on the New Earth; thus, fish would be excluded from the afterlife. The verse states, "Then I saw a new heaven and a new earth, for the first heaven and the first earth had passed away, and the sea was no more." However, this contradicts the New Earth sea mentioned in Isaiah 11:9. I think Revelation 21:1 means that the sea as we know it now, a hostile and scary body of water, will no longer exist on the New Earth. The scariness of the current sea is presented in Psalm 89:9 and Jeremiah 31:35. This would make sense as Revelation 22:1–2 describes a river on the New Earth. Where would the water flow to if there was no sea for it to empty into? All land but no sea would not accord with Eden restored (Ezekiel 36:35), where God created the seas (Genesis 1:10) and the sea life (Genesis 1:20–22). Thus, we believe fish will also have a place to dwell too on the New Earth, only it will be a peaceful body of water instead.

Question: What about Isaiah 35:9?

Answer: The verse states, "No lion shall be there, nor shall any ravenous beast come up on it; they shall not be found there, but the redeemed shall walk there." This verse is commonly employed to say that animals will not be on the New Earth or even to imply that the lions, and thus all the animals, mentioned in Isaiah 11:6 and 65:25, are metaphors for humans. Isaiah 35:9 is not describing the lions themselves but rather, the lions' carnivorous (1 Peter 5:8) and brutal nature (2 Kings 17:25, Proverbs 28:15) that will no longer be present on the New Earth. This is most explicit in the NASB translation, which uses the word "vicious" instead of the ESV's "ravenous" to describe the beast. This is evident as earlier Isaiah 34:14 describes hyenas peacefully mingling with other wild animals. Hyenas are carnivorous now, but on the future New Earth will be peaceful like the lions mentioned in Isaiah 11:6 and 65:25. Isaiah 34:14 continues with this tranquil imagery to include a goat and a bird finding a resting place. Later, Isaiah 35:7 describes jackals resting in a restored habitat, which contains harmless plants where there were previously thorns, nettles, and thistles (Isaiah 34:13). Thus, Isaiah 35:9 further implies that there will be no meat or death on the New Earth, not even for previously carnivorous animals like lions and hyenas.

Ezekiel 34:25 has a similar expression, as the verse states that wild beasts will be banished from the land. This means that the animals' brutal nature will be banished, not the creatures themselves. Verse 34:28 confirms this, stating that the beasts of the land will no longer devour humans. This also points to animals on the New Earth being friendly and no longer predatory.

Question: Is There Enough Room on the New Earth for All the Resurrected Bodies?

Answer: Housing all the humans of faith who will be resurrected plus all of the animals will require a sizeable amount of real estate. In addition, animals may even breed on this New Earth, as Isaiah 34:14–17 prophesies. Verse 15 indicates that owls will lay eggs and gather their hatched young. Verse 17 points to the New Earth as it speaks of an eternal dwelling place for animals. Although, this may not mean continued reproduction. Perhaps these are only owls that died on this earth before they could lay their fertilized eggs. They would then resume this birthing process on the New Earth. Regardless, it is reasonable to acknowledge that there is no way that we would all fit on the current earth, let alone be able to have enough resources.

Who says the New Earth will be the same size as the old earth? Revelation 21:9–27 discusses the New Jerusalem, a celestial paradisaical city that will descend upon the New Earth. Revelation 21:16 describes the city as being 12,000 stadia in length, width, and height. A stadion is about 607 feet, which calculates to the city alone being roughly 1,380 miles in length, width, and height, and that is just one city! Perhaps God will expand the New Earth to the size of the rest of the Milky Way Galaxy. Perhaps our concept of space and time will be different. The possibilities to make it work are endless.

Question: Are Dogs Excluded from the New Earth?

Answer: This question is derived from Revelation 22:15, which implies that dogs are excluded from the Holy City, New Jerusalem, and thus, the New Earth. Calling a human a "dog" could be describing them as a gentile (like the Canaanite/Syrophoenician woman in Matthew 15:26 and Mark 7:27, respectively), a male prostitute (Deuteronomy 23:18), or a Judaizer (Philippians 3:2), which are Christians falsely teaching that following Jewish customs is obligatory for salvation. In context, Revelation 22:15 is not talking about the literal animal, but rather about some unrepentant sinful human. This fits with the descriptions of Revelation 21:8.

Question: Is Matthew 6:10 Interpreted Differently from Your Understanding of the Verse?

Answer: Matthew 6:10 states, "Your kingdom come, your will be done, on earth as it is in heaven." The verse seems simple on the surface, but digging deeper can lead to head-scratching. Much of how scholars view this verse depends on how they interpret eschatology, the study of the end times. Let me explain my understanding of the verse.

As previously mentioned, I primarily view the Bible through the lens of postmillennialism. I believe Jesus will return in-the-flesh to our current, cursed earth in the end times to establish his reign and usher in an eternal paradise. Thus, I understand Matthew 6:10 to mean "make the conditions on earth more like the conditions of heaven." Earth is our present world, and heaven is the eternal New Earth (Isaiah 65:17, Revelation 21:1). An obvious objection to this is that certain things done in heaven are vastly different and unrealistic from our lives in this current world. For instance, Jesus said marriage, as we know it, does not exist on the New Earth (Matthew 22:30, Mark 12:25, Luke 20:35). Does Matthew 6:10 advocate that we should not marry now?

I would advocate living by Matthew 6:10 based on what the Spirit of the verse is. Jesus probably meant we should strive to live on earth with the same measure of justice God has intended for eternity, based on practicality and potential. We should try and match our world to the New Earth that 2 Peter 3:13 calls a place where righteousness dwells. Thus, each issue would have to be considered on a case-by-case basis. Marriage, among many reasons, primarily exists for procreation (Genesis 1:28, 9:1, 9:7) and dealing with sexual urges (1 Corinthians 7:1–9). On the New Earth, there is no more death (Revelation 21:4), and presumably, there are no sexual urges. Marriage was sanctioned from the beginning (Genesis 2:24), but would be unnecessary on the New Earth. We do not have to address marriage during our time here on earth because some issues will have to wait until Jesus returns to be fully realized. However, we should try our best to create a world without mourning, crying, or pain (Revelation 21:4).

God often accomplishes his will by using his believers as his instruments (Philippians 1:6; 2:13; Hebrews 13:21). With prayer and humble obedience, believers can help enact God's will on earth, as evidenced by the fruit of the Spirit in Galatians 5:22–23. These verses indicate that anything with love, joy, peace, patience, kindness, goodness, faithfulness, gentleness, and self-control is guided by the Holy Spirit. Being kind to animals reflects all of these nine principles. We can also be sure of the Holy Spirit working in believers to accomplish God's will by looking at his ultimate will in Eden and on the New Earth. If we notice something resembling both Eden and the New Earth that can be practically and realistically done to advance God's kingdom, then we can feel confident in accomplishing the task as an instrument of God. This will honor (1 Corinthians 6:20) and please (Philippians 2:13) him and his work in restoring the world. It is important to note; these actions have nothing to do with salvation, which is through our faith and God's grace alone (Ephesians 2:8). Rather, these works represent the ultimate will of God. We must be careful about always following through with the will of God in a peaceful manner. History is stained with the blood shed by political regimes that thought they could immanentize the eschaton or bring a societal utopia to earth.

Thus, my interpretation of Matthew 6:10 is that we as humans should try our best to implement justice as practically and peacefully as possible, so that all of creation will experience God's goodness (Psalm 34:8) and righteousness (Matthew 6:33). Jesus calls believers to be the light of the world (Matthew 5:14), which again, I interpret as being the solution to the world's problems. Seeking justice and righteousness for the world shines a light in the darkness of cruelty and affliction and ultimately gives glory to our Father in heaven (Matthew 5:16). Humans and animals will live in harmony on the New Earth (Isaiah 11:6–9, 65:25; Hosea 2:18). Thus, we should help implement that as much as practically possible.

Critics of my interpretation often state that Matthew 6:10 simply means that believers are to follow God's will without opposition, but that aligns with my interpretation, as well. What is God's ultimate will? We see in Isaiah and Hosea that his will includes peaceful harmony between all species, a restoration of Eden. The Christian Animal Rights Association advocates implementing NEA to help believers to become instruments of God's ultimate will.

Question: Are the Prophecies of Isaiah Only about the Millennium?

Answer: Christians often reject the idea of animals being on the eternal New Earth, declaring that the passages about peaceful animals in Isaiah 11:6–9 and 65:25 are about the millennium. However, this would be inconsistent with the concept of Eden restored (Revelation 22:1–5), as animals most certainly were present in Eden (Genesis 2:19–20). Some scholars believe Isaiah 11:6–9 only speaks of the millennium, stating that the animals mentioned are simply allegories for different personalities of humans. Wolves dwelling with lambs is understood to mean aggressive humans growing to care for docile humans, respectively. This allegory could be intended in a broader scope, but the primary reference is to animals as the New Earth will be a restoration of Eden. Another possible reason this section is interpreted as only speaking of the millennium is that there are mentions of children (verses 6 and 8). Second Samuel 12:22-23 indicates that the souls of deceased earthly children are in the current spiritual heaven. Perhaps these children in the eternal state will resume the age they were when they died. Another possibility is that these children are symbolic of believers at any age, as Jesus tells us to become like children to enter the kingdom (Matthew 18:3, 19:14; Mark 10:15; Luke 18:17). The Bible is not explicit about whether we will age or not on the New Earth. I imagine age will not matter, as we will all probably feel youthful and have vitality. I remember when I was 25, I was in the best shape of my life. Maybe I'll be 25 again, only this time eternally!

Isaiah 65:17-25 is a confusing set of verses. Some scholars believe the entire section is talking about the millennium, which would exclude animals (65:25) from the afterlife. Isaiah 65:17 has God stating, "For behold, I create new heavens and a new earth, and the former things shall not be remembered or come into mind." Isaiah 65:18-19 describes eternal joy and no more sadness on the New Earth. However, verses 20-23 seem to jump back to the millennium by speaking of children being born (possibly verse 20 and definitely verse 23). Yet, Jesus stated that marriage, as we know it, will no longer exist on the New Earth (Matthew 22:30, Mark 12:25, Luke 20:35), which would imply no sex, and thus no children. Similarly, death will exist as a man will be considered young when he dies at 100 (verse 20), and humans will live as many days as a tree (verse 22). Trees live a long time but eventually die, so this cannot be about the New Earth, where there is no more death (Revelation 21:4). Verses 20-23 must be about the millennial kingdom that will be established through the church by the Holy Spirit, which will improve all dimensions of life.

Isaiah then comes back to the New Earth in 65:24 as it mentions prayers being answered before they are fully stated. Then 65:25 states that animals will live peaceably together on the holy mountain. We can know Isaiah 65:17-19, 24, and 25 are about the New Earth because these verses correspond with Revelation

21:4's description of the New Earth, which says there will be no death, mourning, crying, or pain anymore. Similar to the Old Testament prophecies about Jesus, such as Zechariah 9:9–10, the writer of Isaiah 65:17–25 is employing a literary device known as prophetic foreshortening. Since we just finished discussing God's holy mountain, the best illustration is the image of a mountain. When a prophet has a vision of the future, they sometimes see events that appear to have proximity to one another. The prophet sees future events all as one event, with no clear measure of time between them. However, the prophet is only seeing the peaks and cannot tell that there is a sizable distance between the mountains, the same way the events are farther apart in time than described in the text. Thus, Isaiah 65:20–23 describes God gradually improving the world in the millennial kingdom. Then God will restore it entirely on the finished New Earth in Isaiah 65:17–19 and 65:24–25. Perhaps this illustration will help.

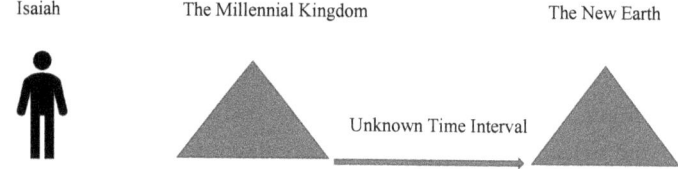

11

Questions about Individual Passages

Question: What about Romans 14:1-3?

ANSWER: THIS PASSAGE STATES, "As for the one who is weak in faith, welcome him, but not to quarrel over opinions. One person believes he may eat anything, while the weak person eats only vegetables. Let not the one who eats despise the one who abstains, and let not the one who abstains pass judgment on the one who eats, for God has welcomed him."

This passage is often used to justify eating meat. It is commonly thought that Paul is criticizing vegans and vegetarians by calling them weak. Due to food access at the time, I am not sure there was such a thing as a vegetarian during droughts or crop devastation. Paul was a devout Jew who knew the Old Testament well (Philippians 3:5). He knew that God had initially prescribed veganism (Genesis 1:29), the health benefits of Daniel's diet (Daniel 1:1-21), and the future vegan diet implied on the New Earth (Isaiah 11:6-9; Isaiah 65:25; Hosea 2:18). Thus, it would have been unlikely for him to criticize what God advocated for and thought was ideal.

Paul wrote this verse when the early church was divided over whether to eat the flesh of animals that had been sacrificed to idols.

To diffuse this quarrel, Paul said the conflicting sides should accept each other's opinions and should not fight about it. The issue becomes clear when reading 1 Corinthians, where Paul addresses the believers in Corinth about the same issue. The weak in faith were not vegans or vegetarians, but rather, those whose conscience could not tolerate the idea that they would be supporting idols with their food purchases and ingestion (1 Corinthians 8:7). Paul declares it an irrelevant issue in 1 Corinthians 8:8.

It is further evident that Paul is talking about animals sacrificed to idols (demons) in 1 Corinthians 10. Verse 14 states, "Therefore, my beloved, flee from idolatry." Then, 10:19–20 states, "What do I imply then? That food offered to idols is anything, or that an idol is anything? No, I imply that what pagans sacrifice they offer to demons and not to God. I do not want you to be participants with demons." Then in 10:25, Paul says, "Eat whatever is sold in the meat market without raising any question on the ground of conscience." Finally, in 10:28, "But if someone says to you, 'This has been offered in sacrifice,' then do not eat it, for the sake of the one who informed you, and for the sake of conscience." These passages have nothing to do with the morality behind how or why animals are farmed or killed, but rather they refer to a specific issue that is not really applicable today.

Question: What about 1 Corinthians 9:9–10?

Answer: This passage is commonly weaponized to show that God does not care about animals. The verses state, "For it is written in the Law of Moses, "You shall not muzzle an ox when it treads out the grain." Is it for oxen that God is concerned? Does he not certainly speak for our sake? It was written for our sake, because the plowman should plow in hope and the thresher thresh in hope of sharing in the crop."

In context, this passage is talking about Paul declaring it acceptable for Christian ministers to receive compensation for preaching the gospel (1 Corinthians 9:14). Upon first reading, this passage makes a seemingly arrogant statement. It seems Paul is stating the original verse, Deuteronomy 25:4, was not intended for oxen, but rather was written for humans all along. However, pondering further, it appears Paul is not nullifying the previous law about allowing the oxen to eat the grain they work, but rather he is building upon the principle of the verse. The theme of Deuteronomy 25:4 is that it is cruel not to let the oxen eat some of what they work to produce. The first question is answered with an undeniable affirmation. Paul then asserts with the second question that if God cares for animals with this principle, it should also be considered for humans. Paul uses the concept of oxen sustaining themselves with the fruits of their hard work to justify Christian ministers also sustaining themselves with the money they gain from preaching. This point is made even more evident in 1 Timothy 5:18.

I was inspired by the *HuffPost* article, "What's St. Paul's Beef With Oxen? Animal Compassion in Light of 1 Corinthians 9:9-10", by Michael Gilmour.[1] A theological implication of Paul's words is this principle applied explicitly to animals in Deuteronomy 25:4 can also broadly apply to humans. Then would not verses explicitly addressing humans also broadly apply toward some issues with animals? Consider the many verses that include both humans and animals in issues like the afterlife (Psalm 36:6), satisfaction (Psalm 145:16), and pity (Jonah 4:11). Based on Paul's handling of Deuteronomy 25:4, it is not a stretch of the text to apply the principles of the Golden Rule and the Second Great Commandment to animals as well as to humans. Once this inclusion has been made, it is evident that many verses about protecting vulnerable humans (Psalm 82:3-4, Proverbs 24:11, Proverbs 31:8-9) could also, in principle, be applied to animals.

1. Gilmour, "St. Paul's Beef with Oxen?"

Question: What about Colossians 2:16?

Answer: This verse states, "Therefore let no one pass judgment on you in questions of food and drink, or with regard to a festival or a new moon or a Sabbath."

In context, Paul is not talking about the ethics of meat here, but rather that Christians are not bound to Jewish cultural laws established in the Old Testament, such as following kosher dietary restrictions (Leviticus 11:1–47; Deuteronomy 14:3–21), holidays (Leviticus 23:34), or observing the Sabbath (Exodus 20:8).

Question: What about 1 Timothy 4:1-3?

Answer: This passage states, "Now the Spirit expressly says that in later times some will depart from the faith by devoting themselves to deceitful spirits and teachings of demons, through the insincerity of liars whose consciences are seared, who forbid marriage and require abstinence from foods that God created to be received with thanksgiving by those who believe and know the truth."

This passage is commonly cited against vegans and vegetarians to fit the ominous description. However, it is important to note that the verses state these false teachers are those who require abstinence from foods *and* forbid marriage. That part about marriage dismisses vegan ideology as the supposed false teachings, since no mainstream vegan organization that we know of advocates the prohibition of marriage. The verse's description of false teachers matches that of Gnosticism, a rival movement in biblical times. Gnosticism was considered a Christian heresy, and some of the teachings were ascetic as followers were taught to avoid marriage and certain types of food. This is confirmed later in the letter as 1 Timothy 6:20 displays Paul criticizing those who babble about "knowledge." The original Greek word for knowledge reads *gnōseōs*, the root word for Gnosticism.

12

Questions about Nephesh Personhood

Question: Are Insects Persons?

ANSWER: THERE IS DEBATE about whether insects qualify as *nephesh chayyah*. Many insects are mentioned in the Bible, like hornets (Exodus 23:28; Deuteronomy 7:20; Joshua 24:12), gnats (Exodus 8:16–17), grasshoppers (Leviticus 11:22; Ecclesiastes 12:5), crickets (Deuteronomy 28:42), and moths (Job 4:19; Isaiah 51:8). None of these creatures are ever designated a *nephesh chayyah*.

To recap, Genesis 1:20 designates *nephesh chayyah* to fish, and 1:21 assigns *nephesh chayyah* to great sea creatures. Genesis 1:20–21 implies *nephesh chayyah* toward birds (later confirmed in Genesis 1:30 and 2:19–20). Genesis 1:24 attaches *nephesh chayyah* to livestock, creeping things, and beasts of the earth. Genesis 1:30 then declares all previously mentioned animals as having *nephesh chayyah*. Genesis 2:7 assigns *nephesh chayyah* to humans. Finally, Genesis 2:19–20 attributes *nephesh chayyah* to livestock, birds, and beasts of the field.

One substantial indicator of *nephesh* is discussed in Leviticus 17:11, which links the term to blood. Insects do not have red blood cells like the creatures definitively declared *nephesh chayyah*. However, insects do have hemolymph, an analogous blood-like substance. Without a definitive answer, it is probably best to give insects a courtesy consideration in personhood, especially since research has discovered that insects too possess unique personalities.[1] Thus, they also should not be treated as property or be exploited. Humans should strive to live harmoniously with them by showing considerations of equality and servanthood. This is why the Christian Animal Rights Association, by utilizing the principles of NEA, advocates to refrain from ingesting honey or carmine, which are products made from the exploitation of bees and cochineal insects, respectively.

Similarly, other invertebrates are described several times in the Bible, like spiders (Job 8:14; Isaiah 59:5), scorpions (Deuteronomy 8:15; Ezekiel 2:6), and worms (Exodus 16:20; Isaiah 14:11). These animals are also not designated *nephesh chayyah*. The same courtesy considerations should be given to these creatures. Especially since research indicates, spiders might possess personalities.[2] Since invertebrates may have *nephesh chayyah*; it is best to avoid products like silk.

Question:
What about the Separation of Church and State?

Answer: The Bible makes clear that the authority of the state is different from the authority of God when Jesus states in Matthew 22:21, "Therefore render to Caesar the things that are Caesar's, and to God the things that are God's." This is also stated in Mark 12:17 and Luke 20:25. The question of Christianity's influence on politics is still controversial and highly debated. Many verses indicate Christians are to be obedient to the government (Romans 13:1–7, Titus 3:1, 1 Peter 2:13–17). These verses are often abused to mean Christians should submit to unjust laws. However, Scripture also commends humans who disobeyed unjust laws. Ironically Peter, the author of 1 Peter 2:13–17, disobeyed the Sanhedrin when he

---

1. Collins, "Insects Have Distinct Personalities."
2. Drake, "Spiders May Have Personalities."

continued to preach the gospel, with his justification in Acts 5:29 being, "We must obey God rather than men."

Disobeying the law when it is unjust is acceptable and even encouraged. Exodus 1:15–17 details the Egyptian king telling two midwives, Shiphrah and Puah, to kill all the newborn Hebrew males. The midwives instead let the boys live because they feared God. I argue this is also the case with the property status of animals. The Bible gives us a framework to acknowledge that it is not ideal, and thus Christians should oppose laws that bind animals to property status. Instead, Christians should aim to change the laws for animals and grant them personhood.

13

Questions about NEA

Question: Does Romans 1:25 Condemn NEA?

ANSWER: ROMANS 1:25 STATES, "Because they exchanged the truth about God for a lie and worshiped and served the creature rather than the Creator, who is blessed forever! Amen." This verse could be read as an accusation against NEA as it condemns serving the creature. However, this verse is quote-mined. In context, this verse condemns worshipping graven images, human-made objects also known as idols. Within the same paragraph, the earlier verses, Romans 1:22–23, state, "Claiming to be wise, they became fools, and exchanged the glory of the immortal God for images resembling mortal man and birds and animals and creeping things." This idol worship is condemned throughout the Bible. The most well-known example being one of the Ten Commandments (Exodus 20:4–5). I completely agree with the passage, as we should not create images of animals and worship them. We should, however, serve actual animals as Jesus taught us to be servants of all (Mark 9:35).

QUESTIONS ABOUT NEA

Question: Will Animals Work on the New Earth?

Answer: Upon first reading, Isaiah 30:24 would seem to indicate oxen and donkeys will be property on the New Earth, as it describes them working the ground. This could be read literally, but the descriptions of animals make more sense when read symbolically. The New Earth is most certainly being discussing in Isaiah 30:19 as it describes no more weeping in Jerusalem, but verses 20–25 seem to jump back. Verse 20 prophesies the arrival of Jesus with adversity and affliction for the disciples and apostles as they preach the gospel, with verse 21 describing the Holy Spirit as he guides the ministry. Verse 22 predicts the success of the gospel, as idols and images are destroyed. Verse 23 describes livestock grazing in large pastures, which represents Christian ministers preaching in a new and expanding world. Verse 24 discusses oxen and donkeys eating seasoned fodder, indicating preachers will be paid well for their services. This section is obviously not about the New Earth, as verse 25 discusses slaughter. This section is a prophecy about the church. The animals here could also be interpreted as literal, as they also prosper due to improved ethics when the church spreads.

Question: Does Riding Horses Violate NEA?

Answer: Horseback riding is not mentioned in the garden of Eden. However, in this cursed world, horses have been frequently associated with wars. There are mentions of horses with chariots (Exodus 14:9, Deuteronomy 11:4, Micah 1:13). Horses were often associated with enemy attacks (Exodus 15:1; 1 Samuel 13:5; Isaiah 43:17). Perhaps that is why God commanded Joshua to maim horses, so that they could not be used for battle (11:6; 11:9). David also crippled horses, probably to keep them from being used in war (2 Samuel 8:4; 1 Chronicles 18:4). God seemed to frown upon Israelites using horses (Deuteronomy 17:16; Psalm 20:7; Isaiah 2:7; 31:1). Donkeys were a common form of transportation in biblical times (Genesis 22:3; Judges 5:10; 10:4; 2 Samuel 17:23; 19:26).

I Will Abolish the Bow

Luke 19:35–36 and John 12:14–15 describe Jesus riding a donkey. Camels (Genesis 24:61) and mules (2 Samuel 13:29) were also ridden at the time.

The Bible famously speaks of riding horses in Revelation. However, I do not take these passages to be literal. As a postmillennialist, I approach the passages through a lens of partial preterism, which means that these verses have already occurred. For instance, I believe the horses mentioned in Revelation 9:17 and 14:20 are symbolic of events that are now history. The symbolism makes sense because these horses and their surroundings described are very fantastical. I will provide a few explicit examples. Revelation 6:2 speaks of a white horse with a mounted archer, symbolizing the 67 AD Roman army advancing toward Jerusalem, ready for battle. Revelation 6:4 describes an equestrian on a red horse, symbolizing war in Jerusalem. Revelation 6:5 details a man holding scales while riding on a black horse, which signifies famine resulting from the aforementioned combat (Revelation 6:6). Finally, Revelation 6:8 describes a pale horse, carrying a horseman named Death, which personifies the fatalities from said warfare and starvation.[1] These passages are not all about the past, as some are still symbolically occurring, such as Revelation 19:14. Similarly, Revelation 19:11 portrays a man riding a white horse, which symbolizes Jesus ruling from heaven and through the hearts of the faithful as they Christianize the nations.[2]

Isaiah 66:20 seems to indicate that humanity will use animals for travel on the New Earth. However, at the time this was written, animals were essentially the only form of land transportation available beyond walking, which is unlike today. Thus, perhaps these animals symbolize any means of travel, meaning humans will use cars, planes, and trains instead. Regardless, these will be heavenly horses, mules, and camels who are not liable to injury. This is unlike those same creatures in our fallen world. Horseback riding is dangerous not only for the human, but also for the horse. Riding horses (and other animals) for leisure, though a minor offense,

---

1. Gentry, Jr., "Seven Seals Revelation 6."
2. Rochford, "Postmillennial View."

does not accord with NEA, as it is not serving the animal. To apply the Golden Rule, I would not want to carry someone on my back for a great distance and have a bit shoved in my mouth to control me. Perhaps we will ride horses and other animals on the New Earth, but it will be a restored world, where humans and animals will not risk injury. Maybe even consent could be obtained from them. Until then, our ministry believes it is best to use transportation that does not impose on animals.

Question: Doesn't NEA Discriminate Against Plants?

Answer: Plants may feel pain. However, without a brain or a central nervous system to understand it, can we really call it pain? Humans and nearly all animals have a brain and central nervous system, which not only registers the pain but remembers it and may even obsess over avoiding it. This is known as psychological trauma, which is what is seen in humans and animals with PTSD or learned behaviors of not trusting others. They have been hurt in some way that causes them to develop avoidance behaviors. Does this happen to plants? I doubt it. I am open to the idea, in any case. Say that new research comes out tomorrow that proves we have been wrong all along about plant sentience. They live and experience life, just like humans and animals do. What then? If we cannot wholly avoid harm, then the best thing to do is minimize it. The only logical way to minimize harm in this situation is to continue eating plants. Animals are an incredibly inefficient means of producing food. For every 16 pounds of plants fed to a cow, the cow produces only one pound of meat.[3] A 1,000 lb. cow consumes about 26.5 pounds of dry food each day.[4] In contrast, a typical human ingests around 3 to 4 pounds of food daily.[5] We can significantly reduce the number of supposed plant pain and deaths by just eating plants directly.

3. People for the Ethical Treatment of Animals, "Can Plants Feel Pain?"
4. Ringwall, "BeefTalk: Feed Those Cows."
5. Andrews, "What Are Your 4 Pounds Made of?"

I Will Abolish the Bow

Secular animal rights philosophy has chimed in on the subject, as Tom Regan indicates plants are not subjects-of-a-life, implying they lack fundamental ethical rights.[6] Gary L. Francione of Animal Rights: The Abolitionist Approach concludes similarly, citing that plants lack sentience.[7] Finally, plants were the food source in the garden of Eden in Genesis 1:29–30, and 2:9. Plants are still the food source on the New Earth as implied by Revelation 22:2. Plants are not referred to as *nephesh chayyah*, as humans (Genesis 2:7) and animals are (Genesis 1:20, 21, 24, 30; 2:19–20), and thus cannot be considered persons.

I do fear that years or perhaps decades or centuries from now, I will be guilty of the same charges as my peers, of oppressing and trampling on the rights of others, the plants, in order to uphold the rights of humans and animals. I have tried to understand both scientifically and scripturally and have gathered the best evidence I can. I do apologize if I misunderstood plants and oppressed them with the Bible. Of course, without discriminating against plants, I would also have nothing to eat. Nevertheless, we must be good stewards of the earth, as Genesis 2:15 describes God placing Adam in the garden of Eden to cultivate and tend it. Thus, we should not inflict unnecessary harm or wanton devastation and destruction to vegetation, as humans are to be the divinely appointed caretakers of creation.

Question: Why Veganism When God Promised a Land Flowing with Milk and Honey?

Answer: This phrase is initially found in Exodus 3:8. This milk and honey phrase is referenced again in Exodus 13:5, 33:3; Numbers 13:27, 14:8, 16:13; Deuteronomy 6:3, 11:9, 26:9, 26:15, 27:3, 31:20; Jeremiah 11:5, 32:22; Ezekiel 20:6, and 20:15. I used to think this verse was about the promised consumption of the milk of animals and the honey of bees. However, I was enlightened by a website

---

6. Weeks, "Right Of Plants To Evolve."
7. Francione, "Sentience."

titled Swords to Plowshares. A land flowing with milk and honey indicates babies are being born and the bees are busy pollinating the flora, respectively. Thus, God is not advocating the exploitation of animals, but rather, describing the land as having abundant vegetation with all sentient beings flourishing beside their young.[8] This makes sense as Deuteronomy 6:3 mentions multiplying greatly and 11:9 discusses offspring. It may be possible that literal milk and honey are indicated. However, they may be different from what we might expect. For instance, the honey referred to in the Bible may be grape or date syrup.[9] Regardless of the meaning, these verses are still in relation to our current fallen world, not the ideal in Eden (Genesis 1:29) or the implied diet God has planned for us in eternity (Isaiah 11:6).

---

8. Swords To Plowshares, "Flowing with Milk and Honey?"
9. Jewish Virtual Library, "Jewish Concepts: Honey."

Epilogue

IT CAN BE DIFFICULT being a secular animal rights activist and constantly seeing Christians refuse to extend the mercy and compassion their God so clearly advocates. I hope this book offers you solace in knowing that the Bible and Christianity as a whole can provide a framework for sympathy and mercy that extends to animals. Similarly, it can be really difficult being a Christian animal rights activist in a non-vegan world. When you hear fellow Christians using the Bible to justify the torture and harm animals needlessly experience every day, it can leave your faith shaken. I hope this book gives you a helpful resource to challenge the speciesism that is rampant within the church and among believers. At first, animal rights can be challenging to accept as a Christian, mostly because we are taught to believe that humans are the only species that matter. If you are a Christian considering animal rights, I hope that this book has provided an informative and sensitive introduction to what the Bible says about animals.

After reading this book, we hope Christians will no longer see animals as property or as commodities, but rather as God sees them: as persons–individuals with a unique personality entitled to lawful moral consideration. We hope that by seeing animals as people, Christianity will be able to eliminate the current track record of exploitation and domination. However, you may have further questions, like why didn't Jesus help animals directly? Why wasn't he more explicit about his teachings including animals? You may ask: Given his divinity, why didn't he just forgo eating the Passover and the fish? I don't have an answer for those questions, yet. Perhaps I will never know. However, I think he laid the foundation and knew his church would, with the help of the Holy Spirit, build on his teachings and principles and help restore the kingdom. He has trusted believers to accomplish his will. Christian Animal Rights Association has accepted Jesus' calling, as we seek to help restore the peaceful world that God has promised for animals in the end times.

Now I have a question for you: Will you join us?

Resources for NEA

Christian Animal Rights Association
Website: christiananimalrights.com

Social Media Links:
Facebook: @christiananimalrights
Instagram: christian_animal_rights_assoc_
Twitter: @Christian_AR_
Pinterest: @ChristianAnimalRightsAssoc

Veganism

MODERN ANIMAL AGRICULTURE IS shockingly cruel. To avoid exploiting these farmed animals, it is best to implement a vegan diet. This is a diet free of all animal-derived products, including meat, eggs, dairy, and honey. Don't focus on what you lose but rather what you gain in the many plant-based options available.

Many delicious and healthy recipes can be found:

PETA Recipes—https://www.peta.org/recipes/type/all/

I Love Vegan—https://www.ilovevegan.com/complete-recipe-index/

Experimentation

Animals are experimented on in research and pharmaceutical labs to test effectiveness for human treatments. These methods are outdated and cruel. There are many effective alternatives that do not exploit animals that the industry can integrate. This is primarily a legislative issue.

Organizations that work to end the use of experimentation on animals in the sciences:

American Anti-Vivisection Society (AAVS)—https://aavs.org

National Anti-Vivisection Society (NAVS)—https://www.navs.org

Shopping Cruelty-Free

Animals are experimented on for household products; often to avoid possible litigation. Several companies specialize in creating products made without testing on animals.

Cruelty-Free Products can be found:

Cruelty Free International—https://www.crueltyfreeinternational.org

PETA—https://features.peta.org/cruelty-free-company-search/index.aspx

Cruelty-Free Fashion

Animals are exploited for their fur, skin, and feathers.
There are many alternatives that can be found:

Farm Sanctuary—https://www.farmsanctuary.org/vegan-fashion/

PETA—https://how-to-wear-vegan.peta.org

Resources for NEA

Sanctuaries

Instead of visiting zoos and circuses that often profit from keeping the animals for human spectacle, the Christian Animal Rights Association, utilizing the principles of NEA, advocates visiting non-profit farm sanctuaries instead. The concern for the animals at sanctuaries is of the utmost importance, not the entertainment of humans seen in zoos and circuses.

Farm Animal Sanctuary Directory—https://vegannavigator.com/farm-sanctuaries/

Vegan Dog Food Listings

Our dogs have been eating vegan for five years as of this publication and really enjoy V-dog brand dog food. Here is a comprehensive list of other brands:

https://onlybuyvegan.com/vegan-dog-food/

https://www.peta.org/living/animal-companions/say-kibble-vegan-dog-food-recipe/

> This book provides beneficial information on the matters discussed. However, this book was not intended to detect, remedy, or deter any medical conditions. Additionally, this book was not intended as a replacement for a trained medical professional. Please consult with your physician or veterinarian before implementing any of the suggestions mentioned in this book.

Bibliography

Andrews, Ryan. "What Are Your 4 Pounds Made of? How to Understand Calorie and Energy Density." *Precision Nutrition*, June 17, 2015. https://www.precisionnutrition.com/what-are-your-4-lbs.

Animal Legal Defense Fund. "Animals' Legal Status." 2018. https://aldf.org/issue/animals-legal-status/.

ASPCA. "Pet Statistics." 2015. https://www.aspca.org/animal-homelessness/shelter-intake-and-surrender/pet-statistics.

A-Z Quotes. "Leo Tolstoy Quote." Accessed December 18, 2020. https://www.azquotes.com/quote/355248.

———. "Pythagoras Quote." Accessed December 18, 2020. https://www.azquotes.com/quote/237442.

Barber, Nigel. "How Domestic Animals Succeed in the Wild." *Psychology Today*, November 6, 2019. https://www.psychologytoday.com/us/blog/the-human-beast/201911/how-domestic-animals-succeed-in-the-wild.

Becker, Doug. "Does the Bible Condone Slavery?" *Emergence Church - New Jersey*, January 4, 2019. https://emergencenj.org/blog/2019/01/04/does-the-bible-condone-slavery.

Bekoff, Marc. "After 2,500 Studies, It's Time to Declare Animal Sentience Proven (Op-Ed)." *Live Science*, September 6, 2013. https://www.livescience.com/39481-time-to-declare-animal-sentience.html.

———. "Cows: Science Shows They're Bright and Emotional Individuals." *Psychology Today*, November 2, 2017. https://www.psychologytoday.com/us/blog/animal-emotions/201711/cows-science-shows-theyre-bright-and-emotional-individuals.

———. "Pigs Are Intelligent, Emotional, and Cognitively Complex." *Psychology Today*, June 12, 2015. https://www.psychologytoday.com/us/blog/animal-emotions/201506/pigs-are-intelligent-emotional-and-cognitively-complex.

Bernot, Kate. "New Book 'What Would Jesus Really Eat?' Makes Christian Case for Eating Meat." *The Takeout*, July 19, 2019. https://thetakeout.com/what-would-jesus-really-eat-christian-book-1836530919.

Bibliography

Bible Project, The. "Nephesh: 'Soul.'" Accessed December 19, 2020. https://d1bsmz3sdihplr.cloudfront.net/media/Study%20Notes/WS05-Soul-Final.pdf.

Bloomer, Richard J, et al. "Effect of a 21 Day Daniel Fast on Metabolic and Cardiovascular Disease Risk Factors in Men and Women." *Lipids in Health and Disease* 9, 94. September 3, 2010. https://doi.org/10.1186/1476-511x-9-94.

Braconnier, Deborah. "Sperm Whales Have Individual Personalities." *Phys.org*, March 16, 2011. https://phys.org/news/2011-03-sperm-whales-individual-personalities.html.

Butt, Kyle. "Helping Animals Is Not the Same as Helping People." *Apologetics*, January 1, 2018. https://www.apologeticspress.org/apPubPage.aspx?pub=2&issue=1263&article=2773.

Climate Nexus. "Animal Agriculture's Impact on Climate Change." March 29, 2017. https://climatenexus.org/climate-issues/food/animal-agricultures-impact-on-climate-change/.

Cline, Austin. "Slavery and Racism in the Bible." *Learn Religions*, March 25, 2018. https://www.learnreligions.com/the-bible-race-and-slavery-3893539.

Cobb, David. "Women's 'Legal Personhood' and the 19th Amendment." *Times-Standard*, August 10, 2006. https://www.times-standard.com/2006/08/10/womens-legal-personhood-and-the-19th-amendment/.

Collins, Catherine. "Even Insects Have Distinct Personalities—Research Finds." *Horizon: The EU Research & Innovation Magazine*, May 3, 2016. https://horizon-magazine.eu/article/even-insects-have-distinct-personalities-research-finds.html.

Dictionary.com, LLC. "Definition of Personhood" *Dictionary.com*. Accessed December 18, 2020. https://www.dictionary.com/browse/personhood?s=t.

Drake, Nadia. "Spiders May Have Personalities, and Some Are Bolder Than Others." *Wired*, July 30, 2013. https://www.wired.com/2013/07/social-spiders/.

Famous People, The. "40 Top Jefferson Davis Quotes That Reflect His Mind." Accessed December 19, 2020. https://quotes.thefamouspeople.com/jefferson-davis-1795.php.

Francione, Gary L. "Believe in Animal Rights? Be Prepared to Go Pet-Free." Interview by The 180, CBC News. *CBC/Radio-Canada*, September 16, 2016. https://www.cbc.ca/radio/the180/facts-vs-values-in-canadian-health-care-forced-psychiatric-care-and-urban-indigenous-people-need-a-voice-1.3764173/believe-in-animal-rights-be-prepared-to-go-pet-free-1.3765424

———. "Our Hypocrisy." *New Scientist*, June 4, 2005. https://www.abolitionistapproach.com/media/links/p8/similar-minds.pdf.

———. "Quotes." *Animal Rights: The Abolitionist Approach*. Accessed December 20, 2020. https://www.abolitionistapproach.com/quotes/.

———. "Sentience." *Animal Rights: The Abolitionist Approach*, July 12, 2012. https://www.abolitionistapproach.com/sentience/.

Bibliography

Gammill, Justin. "With Over 200,000 Species of Edible Plants, Why Do Humans Only Consume 200?" *I Heart Intelligence*, March 21, 2016. https://iheartintelligence.com/plants-consume/.

Gentry, Jr., Kenneth L. "The Seven Seals of Revelation 6." *Postmillennial Worldview*, October 1, 2019. https://postmillennialworldview.com/2019/10/01/the-seven-seals-of-revelation-6/.

Gilmour, Michael. "What's St. Paul's Beef with Oxen? Animal Compassion in Light of 1 Corinthians 9:9-10." *HuffPost*, March 21, 2012. https://www.huffpost.com/entry/whats-st-pauls-beef-with-_b_1216164.

Hess, Ann. "Eating Meat Should Not Be Question of Conscience." *National Hog Farmer*, July 19, 2019. https://www.nationalhogfarmer.com/business/eating-meat-should-not-be-question-conscience.

Holy Comforter-Saint Cyprian Roman Catholic Church. "What Sorts of Food Were Common in the Time of Jesus?" Accessed December 19, 2020. https://hcscchurch.org/wp-content/uploads/2014/08/food.pdf.

ISRAEL21c Staff. "Turns out Mice Have Personality, and Now There's a Way to Measure It." *ISRAEL21c*, November 10, 2019. https://www.israel21c.org/turns-out-mice-have-personality-and-now-theres-a-way-to-measure-it/.

Jackson, Wayne. "What about those Gadarene Hogs?" *Christian Courier*. Accessed December 19, 2020. https://www.christiancourier.com/articles/1011-what-about-those-gadarene-hogs.

Jewish Virtual Library. "Agriculture in Israel: Famine & Drought." Accessed December 19, 2020. https://www.jewishvirtuallibrary.org/famine-and-drought-in-israel.

———. "Jewish Concepts: Honey." Accessed December 19, 2020. https://www.jewishvirtuallibrary.org/honey.

Keim, Brandon. "What Racism, Sexism and a Belief in Human Superiority Have in Common." *Anthropocene Magazine*, February 21, 2018. https://www.anthropocenemagazine.org/2018/02/psychology-of-speciesism/.

Khamsi, Roxanne. "Lizards Have Personalities Too, Study Shows." *New Scientist*, November 8, 2006. https://www.newscientist.com/article/dn10473-lizards-have-personalities-too-study-shows/.

Knowles, Hannah, and Katie Mettler. "Trump Signs a Sweeping Federal Ban on Animal Cruelty." *The Washington Post*, November 25, 2019. https://www.washingtonpost.com/science/2019/11/25/most-animal-cruelty-isnt-federal-crime-that-changes-monday-when-bipartisan-bill-becomes-law/.

Langston, Jennifer. "One Day, a Gorilla Touched Her Soul." *Seattle Post-Intelligencer*, April 16, 2004. https://www.seattlepi.com/local/article/One-day-a-gorilla-touched-her-soul-1142523.php.

Legal Information Institute. "Legal Person." *Cornell Law School*. Accessed December 19, 2020. https://www.law.cornell.edu/wex/legal_person.

———. "Natural Person." *Cornell Law School*. September 10, 2009. https://www.law.cornell.edu/wex/Natural_person.

Lexico.com. "Partiality." Lexico Dictionaries | English. Accessed December 20, 2020. https://www.lexico.com/en/definition/partiality.

Bibliography

———. "Person." Lexico Dictionaries. Accessed December 20, 2020. https://www.lexico.com/en/definition/person.

———. "Sentient." Lexico Dictionaries. Accessed December 19, 2020. https://www.lexico.com/en/definition/sentient.

Linzey, Andrew. *Animal Theology*. Chicago: University Of Illinois Press, 1995.

———. *Christianity and the Rights of Animals*. Eugene, OR: Wipf & Stock, 2016.

Lyons, Eric. "The God-Approved View of Animals." *Apologetics*, January 1, 2018. https://www.apologeticspress.org/DiscoveryPubPage.aspx?pub=2&issue=1263.

MacArthur, John. "Putting Humans in Their Place." *Grace to You*, April 20, 2010. https://www.gty.org/library/blog/B100420/putting-humans-in-their-place.

McKie, Robin. "Biologists Think 50% of Species Will Be Facing Extinction by the End of the Century." *The Guardian*, February 25, 2017. https://www.theguardian.com/environment/2017/feb/25/half-all-species-extinct-end-century-vatican-conference.

Melina, Vesanto, et al. "Position of the Academy of Nutrition and Dietetics: Vegetarian Diets." *Journal of the Academy of Nutrition and Dietetics* 116, no. 12. December 1, 2016. https://doi.org/10.1016/j.jand.2016.09.025.

Menikoff, Aaron. "How and Why Did Some Christians Defend Slavery?" *The Gospel Coalition*, February 24, 2017. https://www.thegospelcoalition.org/article/how-and-why-did-some-christians-defend-slavery/.

Merriam-Webster.com Dictionary. "abolition," accessed December 19, 2020, https://www.merriam-webster.com/dictionary/abolition.

———. "Speciesism." accessed December 19, 2020, https://www.merriam-webster.com/dictionary/speciesism.

Miller, Dave. "Humans Are Not Animals." *Apologetics*, 2019. http://www.apologeticspress.org/APContent.aspx?category=7&article=5678.

Morrow, Jonathan. "Only 4 Percent of Gen Z Have a Biblical Worldview." *Impact 360 Institute*, March 2018. https://www.impact360institute.org/articles/4-percent-gen-z-biblical-worldview/.

Mowczko, Marg. "Misogynistic Quotations from Church Fathers and Reformers." *Margaret Mowczko*, January 24, 2013. https://margmowczko.com/misogynist-quotes-from-church-fathers/.

New Catholic Encyclopedia. "Person (In Philosophy)." *Encyclopedia.com*. Accessed December 19, 2020. https://www.encyclopedia.com/religion/encyclopedias-almanacs-transcripts-and-maps/person-philosophy

Newkey-Burden, Chas. "Yes, I Know You Love Bacon—but That's No Excuse for the Things We Do to Pigs." *The Independent*, October 8, 2019. https://www.independent.co.uk/voices/bacon-pigs-meat-industry-animal-cruelty-slaughter-vegan-a9147101.html.

Nonhuman Rights Project. "Litigation." October 6, 2020. https://www.nonhumanrights.org/litigation/.

BIBLIOGRAPHY

O'Neill, Maggie. "Research Reveals Elephants Have Distinct Personalities." *MailOnline*, February 21, 2018. https://www.dailymail.co.uk/sciencetech/article-5418853/Research-reveals-elephants-distinct-personalities.html.

People for the Ethical Treatment of Animals. "Can Plants Feel Pain?" July 7, 2010. https://www.peta.org/about-peta/faq/what-about-plants/.

Petre, Alina. "16 Studies on Vegan Diets — Do They Really Work?" *Healthline*, March 20, 2020. https://www.healthline.com/nutrition/vegan-diet-studies.

Piatek, Gary H. "Salamanders with Personality." *Central Michigan University*, February 22, 2018. https://www.cmich.edu/news/article/pages/Salamander-research.aspx.

Pinker, Steven. *The Better Angels of Our Nature: Why Violence Has Declined*. New York: Penguin, 2012. https://www.pdfdrive.com/the-better-angels-of-our-nature-e60345040.html.

Piper, Kelsey. "Farms Have Bred Chickens So Large That They're in Constant Pain." *Vox*, September 23, 2020. https://www.vox.com/future-perfect/21437054/chickens-factory-farming-animal-cruelty-welfare?fbclid=IwAR1_j39mKHZ38YqzjZNvKS3WfSjwVAUaDzotHxwpn1-31rjoV8qJTlSvbGc.

Psychology Today. "Personality." 2019. https://www.psychologytoday.com/us/basics/personality.

Raja, Vidya. "All Animals Are 'Legal Persons', Court Declares: Here's What It Means." *The Better India*, June 8, 2019. https://www.thebetterindia.com/185543/animal-rights-india-court-judgement-cruelty-prevention/.

Regan, Tom. "Tom Regan, Subject-Of-A-Life. Interview by Caryn Hartglass." *Responsible Eating and Living*, February 21, 2017. https://responsibleeatingandliving.com/tom-regan-subject-of-a-life/.

Ringwall, Kris. "BeefTalk: Feed Those Cows the Right Amount of Feed." *AgWeb*, February 16, 2015. https://www.agweb.com/article/beeftalk-feed-those-cows-the-right-amount-of-feed-NAA-university-news-release.

Rochford, James M. "3. Postmillennial View: We Initiate the 1,000 Years." *Evidence Unseen*. Accessed December 19, 2020. http://www.evidenceunseen.com/theology/eschatology/3-postmillennial-view-we-initiate-the-1000-years/.

Samuel, Dave. "Do Individual Whitetail Bucks Have Different Personalities?" *Grand View Outdoors*, August 21, 2019. https://www.grandviewoutdoors.com/whitetail-deer/do-individual-whitetail-bucks-have-different-personalities.

Samuel, Sigal. "The Meat We Eat Is a Pandemic Risk, Too." *Vox*, Aug 20, 2020. https://www.vox.com/future-perfect/2020/4/22/21228158/coronavirus-pandemic-risk-factory-farming-meat.

Sanders, Bas. "Global Animal Slaughter Statistics And Charts." *Faunalytics*, October 10, 2018. https://faunalytics.org/global-animal-slaughter-statistics-and-charts/.

BIBLIOGRAPHY

Shooster, Jay. "Legal Personhood and the Positive Rights of Wild Animals." *Wild-Animal Suffering Research*, July 11, 2017. https://was-research.org/writing-by-others/legal-personhood-positive-rights-wild-animals/.

Singer, Peter. *Animal Liberation*. New York: Avon, 1977.

Smith, Wesley J. "Animal Rights Means No Dogs and Cats." *National Review*, September 9, 2016. https://www.nationalreview.com/corner/animal-rights-means-no-dogs-and-cats/.

Springer. "Think Chicken: Think Intelligent, Caring, and Complex." *ScienceDaily*. January 3, 2017. www.sciencedaily.com/releases/2017/01/170103091955.htm

Strieker, Gary. "Researchers Uncover Africans' Part in Slavery." *CNN*, October 20, 1995. http://edition.cnn.com/WORLD/9510/ghana_slavery/.

Swords To Plowshares. "What Does It Mean in Ezekiel 20:6 for a Land to Be Flowing with Milk and Honey?" February 3, 2019. https://swords2plowshares.com/what-does-it-mean-in-ezekiel-206-for-a-land-to-be-flowing-with-milk-and-honey/.

Tarico, Valerie. "20 Disgustingly Misogynist Quotes from Religious Leaders." *Salon*, October 15, 2014. https://www.salon.com/2014/10/15/20_disgustingly_misogynist_quotes_from_religious_leaders_partner/.

Taylor, Daron. "Humans Have Changed Industrial Turkeys So Much They Can't Even Mate Without Our Help." *The Washington Post*, November 22, 2016. https://www.washingtonpost.com/news/wonk/wp/2016/11/22/humans-have-changed-industrial-turkeys-so-much-they-cant-even-mate-without-our-help/.

University of Exeter. "Fish Have Complex Personalities, Research Shows." *Phys.org*, September 25, 2017. https://phys.org/news/2017-09-fish-complex-personalities.html.

University of York. "Animals Have Personalities, Too, Bird Study Suggests." *ScienceDaily*. April 28, 2011. www.sciencedaily.com/releases/2011/04/110427092053.htm

Vandenboom, Cameron, et al. "A Deeper Look into Personhood." *Definitions of Personhood*. Accessed December 18, 2020. http://definitions-of-personhood.weebly.com/a-deeper-look-into-personhood.html.

V-dog. "3 Studies on Vegan Diets for Dogs." Accessed December 19, 2020. https://v-dog.com/blogs/v-dog-blog/3-studies-on-vegan-diets-for-dogs?_pos=1.

Waggoner, Kristen. "Let's Talk about Legal 'Personhood.'" *Washington Examiner*, September 1, 2019. https://www.washingtonexaminer.com/opinion/op-eds/lets-talk-about-legal-personhood.

Weeks, Linton. "Recognizing the Right of Plants to Evolve." *NPR*, October 26, 2012. https://www.npr.org/2012/10/26/160940869/recognizing-the-right-of-plants-to-evolve.

Wilson, Andrew. "What About the Pigs?" *Think Theology*, July 5, 2017. https://thinktheology.co.uk/blog/article/what_about_the_pigs.

Subject Index

Abolition, 22–23
   See also New Earth
      Abolition (NEA)
abortion, 2–3, 10
Academy of Nutrition and
   Dietetics, 25
afterlife
   animals immortal souls,
      79–80
   animals in heaven, 78, 84–85
   dogs in heaven, 86
   fish in heaven, 82–84
   heaven on earth, 86–88
   Isaiah prophecies, 88–90
   meat in heaven, 80–82
   resurrected bodies, 85
Animal Agriculture Alliance, 43
Animal Farm (Orwell), 67
Animal Legal Defense Fund, 13
Animal Liberation (Singer), 6
Animal rights
   Christianity and, 5–6
   Christianity's failure in
      addressing, 1–3
   Darwinism and, 3–5
   secular teachings, 6–7
animal rights activists, xi, xiv,
   xv, 22
"Animal Rights Means No Dogs
   and Cats" (Smith), 32
Animal Rights: The Abolitionist
   Approach (website), 22

animal sacrifice, 63–64, 65,
   72–73, 92
animal sanctuaries, 38–40
animal shelters, 34
Animal Theology (Linzey), 48, 58
animals
   bible weaponizing against,
      43, 92–93
   domesticated (*See*
      domesticated animals)
   entertainment, exploited for,
      27–28
   experimentation, exploited
      for, 26
   extinction, 28, 31–32, 35, 37
   fashion, exploited for, 27
   flesh of, 55–58
   food, exploited for, 24–26,
      51
   harmony with, 20–21, 23
   horse riding, 99–101
   immortal souls, possession
      of, 79–80
   Jesus, equal to or serving,
      72–74
   Jesus' teachings applied to,
      68–72
   personalities of, 13–16
   as persons, 12–13
   as property, 60–62
   as resources, 58–60
   self-defense and, 29

Subject Index

animals (*continued*)
    wild animals, xv, 14, 28–29
    working on the New Earth, 99
    See also biblical regulation
anthropocentrism, 35
Augustine, Bishop of Hippo, 44

The Better Angels of Our Nature: Why Violence Has Declined (Pinker), 48
bible
    addressing abuse of, 41–43, 61–62
    not taking Lord's name in vain, 42
    serving others/serving-self, 42
    weaponizing against animals, 43, 92–93
Bible Project, 10
biblical definitions
    animals, as persons, 12–13
    God's cares for animals, 92–93
    humans, as persons, 11
    nephesh personhood, 9–11
    observational evidence, 15–16
    personhood, defining, 8–9
    scientific evidence, 13–15
    secular definitions of personhood, 9
    vegans and vegetarians, 91–92, 94
biblical regulation
    animal flesh, 55–58
    animals, 52–53
    animals as property, 60–62
    animals as resources, 58–60
    overview, 52–53
    slavery, 53–54
birds, personalities of, 14
Boethius, 10
Butt, Kyle, 46

Canadian Broadcasting Corporation (CBC), 31
The Case for Animal Rights (Regan), 6
Catholic Church, 2
cats, 34–35
charity, 5
chickens, personalities of, 14
Christian Animal Rights Association
    animal rights activists and, xi
    Commandment on killing, 72
    on companion animals, 33–34
    on domesticated animals, 37
    formation of, xii, xiii, 3
    honey/carmine ingestion, 96
    Imago Dei and, 47
    on personhood, 7, 13, 21
    principles of, 20, 33, 43, 61–62
    veganism and, 24
Christian Courier, 77
Christian Vegetarian Association, 3
Christianity
    Animal rights and, 5–6
    failure in addressing animal rights, 1–3
    speciesism and, 46
    . *See also* afterlife; Jesus, questions about
Christianity and the Rights of Animals (Linzey), 5
church-state, separation of, 96–97
cognition, partiality and, 49
companion animals, xii, 33–35
creeping things, personalities of, 14
The Crucible (Miller), 67
cruelty-free products, 26–27

Subject Index

Darwin, Charles, 3, 4
Darwinism, 3–5
Davis, Jefferson, 41
Descartes, René, 15
dogs, 32, 33–35, 86
domesticated animals
   abolitionist approach, 31
   companion animals, 33–35
   Francione's approach, 31–32
   future for, 36–38
   ideal approach, 38–39
   language, changing of, 35–36
   presuppositions, 32–33
   realistic approach, 39–40
dominion
   biblical definition, 17
   in context, 17–18
   future prophecies, 20–21
   Golden Rule, 18–19
   Second Great Commandment, 19
   servanthood, 19–20

"Eating meat should not be question of conscience" (Hess), 43
elephants, personalities of, 15
entertainment, animals exploited for, 27–28
environmental impacts, 28
equality, 23
evolutionary theory, 4
Exorcism of the Gerasene Demoniac, 77
experimentation, animals exploited for, 26
exploitation, of animals
   for entertainment, 27–28
   for experimentation, 26
   for fashion, 27
   for food, 24–26
extinction, 28, 31–32, 35, 37

farm sanctuaries, 38–39
fashion, animals exploited for, 27
fatted calf, Jesus' killing of, 67–68
fish, 14, 64, 66–67
fishing, 29
food
   as all are clean, 65–66
   animals exploited for, 24–26, 51
   meat eating, 34–35, 63–65, 101
Fragments on 1 Corinthians (Origen), 41
Francione, Gary L., 9, 22, 31–33, 102
Francis of Assisi, 5
Fuller, Richard, 53–54
future prophecies, 20–21

Gilmour, Michael, 93
Gnosticism, 94
"The God-Approved View of Animals" (Lyons), 43
Golden Rule, 18–19, 23, 69, 93
Good Samaritan, Parable of, 69–70
Great Banquet, Parable of, 81

harmony with animals, 20–21, 23
health benefits of veganism, 25
"Helping Animals is Not the Same as Helping People" (Butt), 46
Hess, Ann, 43
Holy Spirit, fruits of, 87
honey, 96, 102–3
humans
   as persons, 11
   treatment of animals, 23–24
   worth more than animals, 74–76

Subject Index

"Humans are Not Animals" (Miller), 4
hunting, 29

idol worship, 98
Imago Dei (image of God), 46–49
insects as persons, 95–96

Jackson, Wayne, 77
Jamison, Wes, 43
Jesus, questions about
  all foods as clean, 65–66
  drowning pigs, 77
  as equal to or serving animals, 72–74
  fatted calf, killing of, 67–68
  fish eating, 64, 66–67
  humans, worth more than animals, 74–76
  meat eating, 63–65
  teachings applied to animals, 68–72
Jewish Virtual Library, 55
Journal of Personality and Social Psychology, 50

kingdom of heaven/kingdom of God, 80–82
Kook, Abraham Isaac, 48
kosher laws, 57–58, 65–66, 94

lab-grown meat, 34–35
Langston, Jennifer, 9
language, changing of, 35–36
laws, obeying, 96–97
Legal Information Institute, 11, 12
legal persons, 11, 12–13
Linzey, Andrew, 5–7, 48, 58
livestock, personalities of, 14
Lyons, Eric, 43

MacArthur, John, 4
marriage, 86–87, 94

meat eating, 34–35, 63–65, 101
milk and honey, 102–3
Miller, Arthur, 67
Miller, Dave, 4

naming, meaning of, 30
National Hog Farmer (magazine), 43
natural persons, 11
nephesh chayyah (term usage), 10–13, 74, 95–96, 102
nephesh personhood
  biblical definitions, 9–11
  church-state, separation, 96–97
  insects as persons, 95–96
Net, Parable of, 83
New Earth. *See* afterlife
New Earth Abolition (NEA)
  animals, exploited for food, 24–26, 51
  animals work on the New Earth, 99
  companion animals, 33–35
  description of, xiii–xiv, 21
  honey/carmine ingestion, 96, 102–3
  horse riding, 99–101
  Imago Dei and, 47
  plants, discrimination against, 101–2
  principles of, 33
  secular abolition, 22–23
  service to creatures, 98
  tenets of, 23–24
  veganism, 102–3
Nonhuman Rights Project, 13

observational evidence, of personhood, 15–16
On the Origin of Species (Darwin), 4
Origen, 41
Orwell, George, 67

Subject Index

"Our Hypocrisy" (Francione), 32
Parable of the Good Samaritan, 69–70
Parable of the Great Banquet, 81
Parable of the Net, 83
Parable of the Prodigal Son, 67–68
Parable of the Wedding Feast, 80–81
partiality
  Christian speciesism, 46
  cognition and, 49
  defined, 45
  Image of God and, 46–49
  speciesism and, 45–46
Passover, lamb sacrifice, 63–64, 65, 81
personality
  of animals, 13–16
  defined, 13
personhood
  animals, as persons, 12–13
  biblical definitions, 8–16
  humans, as persons, 11
  nephesh personhood (*See nephesh* personhood)
  observational evidence, 15–16
  property status, xii–xiii
  scientific evidence, 13–15
  secular definitions, 9
pigs, 14, 49, 77
Pinker, Steven, 48
plants, discrimination against, 101–2
Prince-Hughes, Dawn, 9
Prodigal Son, Parable of, 67–68
property, animals as, 60–62
property status, xii–xiii
psychological trauma, 101
"Putting Humans in Their Place" (MacArthur), 4
Pythagoras, 50

racism, 45, 50
Regan, Tom, 6–7, 102
reparations, 38–39
rights, welfare and, xii

Salvation Army, 2
scientific evidence, of personhood, 13–15
Second Great Commandment, 19, 23, 69–71, 93
secular abolition, 22–23
secular definitions, 9
secular teachings, 6–7
self-defense, animals and, 29
servanthood, 19–20, 23, 42
serving others/serving-self, 42
sexism, 41, 44–45, 50
Singer, Peter, 6–7
slavery, 11, 36–37, 41
Smith, Wesley J., 32
Social Darwinism, 4–5
souls, 79–80
speciesism
  addressing, 49–51
  Christian speciesism partiality, 46
  cognition partiality, 49
  Image of God partiality, 46–49
  overview, 44
  partiality, 45–46
  racism, 45, 50
  sexism, 41, 44–45, 50
Spirit of the law, 70–72
"St. Paul's Beef With Oxen?" (Gilmour), 93
subjects-of-a-life, 6, 102
Swords to Plowshares (website), 102–3
Syrophoenician Woman's Faith, 71

Tertullian, 44
Thomas Aquinas, 10

Subject Index

Tolstoy, Leo, 50

United States Constitution, 8, 11
United States Supreme Court, 8

veganism, 24–25, 34, 91–92, 94, 102–3

Watson, Donald, 25
Wedding Feast, Parable of, 80–81

welfare, rights and, xii
whales, personalities of, 14
What Would Jesus Really Eat? The Biblical Case for Eating Meat (Jamison), 43
wild animals, xv, 14, 28–29

Young Men's Christian Association (YMCA), 2

Scripture Index

OLD TESTAMENT

Genesis

1:10	84
1:20	12, 14, 102
1:20–21	14, 95
1:20–22	84
1:20–30	xi, 17, 20, 23, 32, 61
1:21	12, 14, 102
1:24	12, 14, 95, 102
1.25	32, 33
1:26	16, 17, 20, 30, 47, 54, 60, 76
1:26–27	10, 46
1:27	76
1:28	87
1:29	55, 58, 91, 103
1:29–30	24, 102
1:30	12, 14–15, 60, 95, 102
1:31	18
2:7	10, 11, 12, 95, 102
2:9	102
2:15	60, 102
2:19	12
2:19–20	14–15, 30, 61, 88, 95, 102
2:24	52, 87
2:25	59
3:6	59
3:7	59
3:16	20
3:17–19	60
3:19	20
3:21	20, 59, 72
4:2	43
4:4	43
4:8	45, 47
4:15	45
5:1	46
6:5	55
6:11	47
6:14–16	76
6:19–20	75
8:11	56
8:20	52, 72
8:21	55
9:1	87
9:1–3	55
9:2	33
9:3	47, 55, 56
9:4	55, 57
9:6	47, 48, 50, 72, 76, 77
9:7	87
9:22–25	45
12:10	55
17:5	30

Scripture Index

Genesis (continued)

17:15	30
21:14	59
22:3	99
24:61	100
26:1	55
27:16	59
32:28	30
41:54	55
43:1	55
49:6	60

Exodus

1:15–17	97
3:8	102
7:13–14	54
7:22	54
8:15	54
8:16–17	95
8:19	54
8:32	54
9:7	52
12:14	57, 63
12:24	57, 63
13:5	102
14:9	99
15:1	99
16	63
16:15	56
16:20	96
16:31	56
20:4–5	98
20:7	42, 43
20:8	94
20:10	43
20:13	71–72
21:2	54
21:16	53
21:26	54
22:31	68
23:28	95
25:4	59
25:5	59
26:14	59

33:3	102
35:7	59
35:23	59
36:19	59
39:34	59

Leviticus

1:9	52, 72
4:3	72
4:14	72
4:28	72
7:26	57
11:1–47	65, 94
11:7	68
11:22	95
13:47–48	59
13:48–49	59
13:52	59
13:59	59
17:3–4	57
17:10	57
17:11	57, 95
17:14	57
19:15	45
19:26	57
23:34	94
24:17–18	48
24:21	48
25:44	53
26:22	xv

Numbers

4:6	59
4:10–12	59
4:14	59
4:25	59
6:6	11
11	63
11:4–6	56
11:18–20	56
11:31–34	56–57, 65, 66
11:34	58
13:27	102

Scripture Index

14:8	102
16:13	102
21:6	xv
31:20	59

Deuteronomy

1:17	45
6:3	102, 103
7:20	95
8:15	96
10:17	46
10:22	11
11:4	99
11:9	102, 103
12:15	57, 58
12:15–16	57
12:20	58
12:23	57
14:3–21	65, 94
15:23	57
16:19	45
17:16	99
18:4	59
22:10	52, 60
22:11	59
23:18	86
24:1	52
25:4	52, 93
26:9	102
26:15	102
27:3	102
28:42	95
31:20	102
32:24	xv

Joshua

11:6	99
11:9	99
24:12	95

Judges

5:10	99
6:37	59

Ruth

1:1	55

1 Samuel

13:5	99
14:32–34	57
15:22	72
16:7	46
16:20	59

2 Samuel

8:4	99
12:22–23	79, 89
13:29	100
17:23	99
19:26	99
21:1	55

1 Kings

21:23	68
22:38	68

2 Kings

1:8	59
3:4	59
8:1	55
9:10	68
17:25	84

1 Chronicles

18:4	99

2 Chronicles

19:7	45

Nehemiah

4:18	29

Job

4:19	95

Scripture Index

Job (*continued*)

5:22–23	xv
8:14	96
20:16	xv
32:19	59
34:19	45

Psalms

7:2	xv
10:9	xv
17:12	xv
20:7	99
22:13	xv
22:16	68
22:20	68
22:21	xv
23	66
34:8	88
36:6	79, 93
49:12–20	79
50:10–11	35
59:14–15	68
68:23	68
72:1–17	18, 75
72:8	18
78:24	63
80:13	68
82:3–4	5, 93
89:9	84
104:24	35
116:6	79
139:13	10
145:16	93

Proverbs

11:17	43
12:10	5, 58, 59, 61, 64
21:3	72
23:20–21	57
24:11	93
24:23	45
27:23	61

28:14	61
28:15	84
28:21	45
31:8–9	5, 93
31:13	59

Ecclesiastes

3:19–21	74
3:21	79
12:5	95
12:7	74, 79

Isaiah

2:7	99
9:6	42
11:6	33, 75, 84, 103
11:6–9	xiii, 21, 23, 24, 33, 61, 78, 88, 91
11:7	82
11:9	81, 84
13:22	xv
14:11	96
20–25	99
25:6	81–82
25:7	82
25:8	20
30:19	99
30:24	99
31:1	99
34:13	84
34:14	84
34:14–17	85
34:15	36
35:5–6	20
35:7	84
35:9	84–85
40:11	66
43:17	99
51:3	20
51:8	95
51:11	80
53:7	72

Scripture Index

56:7	73, 74	34:28	85
59:5	96	36:35	84
60:7	73, 74	40–48	73, 82
65:17	86	43:18–27	73, 74
65:17–19	89, 90	44:11, 73	74
65:17–25	89–90	44:15, 73	74
65:18–19	89	44:23, 73	74
65:20–23	89, 90	44:29–31	73, 74
65:24	89	45:15–25	73, 74
65:24–25	90	46:1–24	73, 74
65:25	xiii, 21, 23, 24, 33, 61, 74, 78, 82, 84, 88, 89, 91	47:10	82, 83
		47:12	83
66:20	100		

Daniel

1:1–21	24–25, 63, 91

Jeremiah

Hosea

1:5	10	2:9	59
8:17	xv	2:18	xiii, 21, 24, 29, 33, 61, 78, 83, 88, 91
9:11	xv		
10:22	xv		
11:5	102	6:6	72
14:1–6	55		
31:35	84		
32:22	102		

Joel

33:18	73, 74	1:1–12	55
49:33	xv		
51:37	xv		

Jonah

52:30	11
4:11	93

Lamentations

Micah

4:9–10	55	1:13	99
		4:8	21, 48

Ezekiel

Zechariah

2:6	96	9:9–10	90
5:17	xv	11:16	67
16:10	59		
20:6	102		
20:15	102		

Malachi

27:18	59	1:3	xv
34:3	59, 67		
34:14	66–67		
34:25	85		

Scripture Index

NEW TESTAMENT

Matthew

3:4	59
4:18–19	66
5:7	18
5:9	18
5:14	1, 61, 88
5:16	88
5:32	52
5:44	70
6:10	21, 24, 48, 61, 76, 86–88
6:26	74, 76
6:33	88
7:6	68
7:12	18, 23, 69
8:11	82
8:28–34	77
9:11	76
9:17	59
10:29	60
10:31	74, 76
12:11	36, 61
12:12	74, 76
13:45–46	68
13:47–50	83
14:13–21	64
15:16–18	65
15:17–18	58
15:22–28	71
15:26	86
16:26	77
18:3	75, 89
18:12–14	66
18:25	68
19:1–12	52
19:8	52
19:9	52
19:14	75, 89
19:19	69
21:12	61
21:12–17	61
22:1–14	80–81
22:2	80
22:21	96
22:30	86, 89
22:37	19
22:39	19, 23, 69
23:11	1
25:40	18, 50
25:45	50
25:46	79, 83
26:21	64
28:18–20	73

Mark

1:6	59
2:16	76
2:22	59
5:1–20	77
6:30–44	64
7:18–20	65
7:19	58
7:24–30	71
7:27	86
9:35	20, 23, 70, 75, 98
10:1–12	52
10:15	75, 89
11:15	61
11:15–19	61
12:17	96
12:25	86, 89
12:31	23, 69
14:18	64
16:15–16	73

Luke

3:6	79
5:4–9	66
5:10	66
5:29	76
5:37–38	59

Scripture Index

6:27	70	3:16	79, 82
6:31	18, 23, 69	4:14	83
7:13	18	4:34	81
8:26–39	77	6:1–15	64
9:10–17	64	6:48	71
10:30–37	69	6:51	83
10:27	23, 69, 71	7:24	46
10:29	69	9:5	1
12:6	60	10:11	66, 72
12:24	74, 76	10:15	67
14:5	60, 69	10:30	20
14:12–24	81	12:14–15	100
14:15	80	13:12–14	19
15:4–7	66	21:5–17	66
15:11–32	67	21:15–17	66
15:23	67		
16:21	68	**Acts**	
17:21	80	5:29	97
18:17	75, 89	10:11–15	58, 65
19:8	38	10:34	45
19:34–36	43	10:38	83
19:35–36	100	10:40–41	64
19:45–48	61	11:4–9	65
20:21	45	20:35	5
20:25	96		
20:35	86, 89		
22:15	64	**Romans**	
22:15–18	81	1:16	71
22:16	81	1:22–23	98
22:19–20	81, 82	1:25	98
23:43	78	2:11	45
24:30	64	6:22	54
24:41–43	64	10:11	59
24:42–43	52	13:1–7	96
		13:9	69
John		14:1–3	91–92
1:1	71	14:14	66
1:29	65	14:17	65–66
1:36	72	14:20	66
1:42	30		
2:13–22	61	**1 Corinthians**	
2:15	61	5:7	65
2:16	61	6:20	87
2:19	73, 82	7:1–9	87

1 Corinthians (continued)

7:15	52
7:21–23	54
8:7–8	92
9:9–10	92–93
9:14	92
10:14	92
10:19–20	92
10:24	2
10:25	52, 92
10:28	92
15:4	73
15:42	78

2 Corinthians

3:6	70
3:16	82

Galatians

3:28	54, 74
5:14	69
5:22–23	83, 87

Ephesians

2:8	87
4:18	52
5:18	70
5:25	82
6:5	54
6:9	54

Philippians

1:6	87
2:3	1, 19
2:3–4	23, 42, 43
2:4	70
2:13	87
3:2	86
3:5	91

Colossians

1:16	35
2:16	58, 94
3:22	54
3:25	45
4:1	54

1 Timothy

1:10	53
4:1–3	94
5:18	93
5:21	45
6:1	54
6:20	94

Titus

2:9	54
3:1	96

Philemon,

1:16	54

Hebrews

3:8	52
4:12	80
4:15	63
8:13	73
9:19	59
9:22	59, 67, 72
10:1–18	72
10:14	74
10:18	73
11:37	59
13:21	87

James

2:1	45
2:9	45

1 Peter

1:17	46
1:19	57
2:13–17	96

Scripture Index

2:18	54	6:4	100		
3:7	74, 75	6:5	100		
3:8	43	6:6	100		
5:8	84	6:8	100		
		6:11	59		
2 Peter		7:9	59		
		9:17	100		
1:11	80	14:20	100		
2:12	79	19:9	82		
2:22	68–69	19:11	100		
3:13	21, 87	19:14	100		
		20:7	73		
1 John		21:1	83–84, 86		
2:6	20	21:4	21, 60, 80, 82, 83, 87, 89–90		
3:5	63–64	21:8	86		
		21:9–27	85		
Jude		21:16, 85			
1:10	79	21:22	73–74		
		22:1–2	84		
Revelation		22:1–5	88		
3:5	59	22:2	83, 102		
4:4	59	22:3	54		
5:13	78	22:14	59		
6:2	100	22:15	86		

www.ingramcontent.com/pod-product-compliance
Lightning Source LLC
Chambersburg PA
CBHW072150160426
43197CB00012B/2325